W9-AWU-967

WHAT PEOPLE ARE SAYING

"*Deliberate Mindset* is clear as can be, engaging, and best of all, wise. It will help you identify your limiting mindsets and construct new ones – at work, at home, or anywhere your mindsets take you."

Douglas Stone
Founder, Triad Consulting Group; Co-author of
Difficult Conversations and *Thanks for the Feedback*

"Our consultants find themselves in high-stakes situations on a regular basis and having a powerful mindset is critical to their success. Sue and Jeff have provided an excellent resource for taking control of one's mindset – a highly valuable resource!"

Chris Petrini-Poli
CEO, HBR Consulting

"This book provides valuable insights into how one can become more grounded and confident in a whole range of high-stakes situations and help to produce positive outcomes. Jeff and Sue have done a great job linking their experience as coaches and professional development leaders into practical tools and stories that are enjoyable to read."

Susan Korn
Vice President, Project Management,
Exelon Corporation

"Jeff and Sue did a very nice job explaining the concepts of mindset and mindset shift and why they are so important for success in the business world. The tools are presented in a clear, user-friendly way to effectively facilitate the shift from a default mindset to a deliberate mindset, setting up for a more positive outcome. The bonus is that the benefit of these skills transcends the business world to all areas of a person's life."

Julie Szekely
Licensed Marriage and Family Therapist and
a member of the IAMFT and AAMFT

DELIBERATE MINDSET

How **thinking differently** can help you succeed
in high-stakes presentations and conversations

JEFF HORNSTEIN AND SUE REYNOLDS-FROST
Foreword by Ruth Reiner

Copyright © 2018

The Speaker's Choice™ TheSpeakersChoice.com

2400 E. Main #103–203, St. Charles, Illinois, 60174

(888) 344-9002

Contents may not be copied, reproduced, or
re-transmitted in part or in whole in print or
electronically without the written permission
of the publisher.

The information and coaching suggestions in this
book should not be used for diagnosis or treatment
nor are they a substitute for professional
psychological care or counseling.

DEDICATIONS

This book is dedicated to my dear friend, confidante, and cherished mentor, Doug Robertson.

His wisdom and guidance caused me to question and ultimately shift my mindset, which in turn helped me change the trajectory of my life in a way I never imagined possible.

I will be eternally grateful for the profound difference he made in my life and the ripple effect it has had on so many others.

I miss you, my friend…your spirit will be with me forever!

~Jeff Hornstein~

To my husband, Angus. My rock and my teacher. Thank you for holding me accountable, for your listening, and unconditional love.

~Sue Reynolds-Frost~

ACKNOWLEDGEMENTS

We have so many people we want to thank for helping us to make this book a reality.

First and foremost, we would like to thank our dear friend and colleague, Pat McCann. Without his nudging, cajoling, and ability to persuade Jeff to start the book, the idea would have been nothing more than a fading thought. Pat not only helped Jeff start the book, but he was also a **major** contributor to it. Thank you, Pat, for all you did to make this a reality.

Next, to our business colleagues, peers, and clients, thank you. Each one of you gave to us graciously as you served as sounding boards for ideas, guinea pigs for techniques, and much-needed critics for content. To our clients, your willingness to push yourselves and shift your mindsets has inspired us time and time again.

To our closest friends and families, many of you have heard us talking about this book for a long (long!) time. You were steadfast in your support and often coached us to continue sticking with it. (In other words, you made us take a dose of our own medicine!) Without your belief, support, feedback, and patience with us, we would not have been able to see this to completion. We are eternally grateful for each and every one of you!

Finally, a very important thank you to two special contributors. To our designer, Amanda Mansk-Perryman:

thank you for your creativity and phenomenal partnership in designing the cover and graphics throughout the book. Secondly, our fastidious and brilliant, internal editor: you know who you are; and we know how meticulous you are. We can only imagine how many hours you spent improving various facets of the book. Without your help, the outcome would have been diminished and we would never have crossed the finish line!

TABLE OF CONTENTS

FOREWORD

More than twenty-five years ago, as a junior management consultant fresh out of business school and shifting from an engineering career, I thought that technical expertise, hard work, and a Harvard MBA would be the keys to my success in this new career. They, of course, helped but were not sufficient. You could even say my overweighting of their importance hindered my ability to build relationships, influence people, and learn the work of a leader. As I moved through different client and project teams, a senior partner and mentor gave me advice that helped me to shift my mindset. He said, "Life is a series of conversations – make them count."

The advice about viewing conversations as a critical and valuable part of life and work stuck with me. In fact, it led me to another career change, toward organization and leadership development. My personal learning and leadership impact increased as I viewed formal, informal, and high-stakes conversations as a key way to influence people, deal with conflict (and try not to generate it), solve problems, and build relationships. The impact we have on people in conversations greatly benefits from setting a deliberate mindset, as Jeff and Sue lay out in this book.

I met Jeff Hornstein eight years ago, during my first week on the job as head of leadership development for University of Chicago Booth School of Business' part-time MBA students. I had been vetting presentation skills coaches to train our students on executive presence. Jeff immediately struck me as one of the most genuine, self-aware, and other-focused consultants I have ever worked with. Over the eight years since I engaged The Speaker's Choice to work with us, Jeff, Sue, and their team always get the highest ratings from our MBA students. Jeff and his team not only consistently model the skills they are teaching, but students always comment on how Jeff's and Sue's non-judgmental, supportive styles help them to shift their confidence and capability in a short time. Their years of experience in industry, consulting, and coaching work extremely well with our highly qualified MBA students. In addition to the presentation skills coaching, Sue and Jeff have worked alongside me and my team to expand and improve our leadership development offerings. In working closely with them, we have developed a deep trust and respect for each other. I have benefited from their insights and, at times, their coaching to help me be a better leader.

I am so glad Sue and Jeff have shared their approach and tools in this book – it is a gold mine. To truly get the most out of their content, I encourage readers to take time to read the book, think of your own examples, and then experiment. Try things out, ask for feedback, reflect, try another approach. Repeat. You should see a payoff quickly.

I am still learning how to be intentional, to pause and consider what impact I want to have. I must keep an open mindset about what I should keep doing, stop doing, or start doing – once I see the impact I've made.

The discipline of maintaining a deliberate mindset and changing the conversations we have with ourselves and with others is a critical leadership skill. As with other skills, mastery requires that we experiment, seek feedback, and reflect. This book provides a great guide to accelerate the process for all leaders.

Ruth L. Reiner, Associate Dean, Leadership Development

Part-time MBA Programs
University of Chicago Booth School of Business

INTRODUCTION

Jeff Hornstein, *CEO & Founder of The Speaker's Choice*

Somehow you've chosen to pick up this book; perhaps someone gave it to you as a gift (or suggested you read it). Maybe you were intrigued by the title, or your interest was piqued as you perused the back cover and table of contents. However this book came into your hands, we are happy it did.

My colleague, Sue Reynolds-Frost, and I wrote *Deliberate Mindset* to compel you to think about the way you think. We wrote this book with the intention of helping you get an edge, so you can be even more successful in high-stakes presentations and conversations than you currently are. By reading this book, we are confident you will learn new ways to shift your mindset and discover ideas, strategies, and approaches to take yourself to another level.

Perhaps you have the goal to demonstrate or embody a higher level of executive presence. If so, do you find yourself challenged by the following types of thoughts?

> *"I really want to develop my communication skills and style, so I can have a more powerful presence, but I'm analytically oriented and somewhat shy which has prevented me from engaging my audiences in the past. How can thinking differently really make a difference? This is just my personality."*

These are the types of thoughts that are linked to a disempowered mindset which could potentially make it difficult to succeed. However, let me assure you, that goal is within your reach. I say that with confidence, because that was me many years ago. A deliberate mindset shift was the launch pad that led me from an unfulfilling career as a manufacturing engineer to my current role as a very fulfilled coach and leader in the field of executive presence and communication training. In fact, I often playfully introduce myself as a "recovering engineer."

When I founded The Speaker's Choice in 2007, I knew a key differentiator for our company would be that we didn't only teach people core presentation skills, i.e., to stand up straight, look people in the eye, and stop saying "um." While these skills, along with several others, are critical, they alone would not differentiate us from any other firm in our field, nor would they propel our clients toward true breakthroughs. Something was missing! The foundation for being able to speak in front of a group, take the personal risks involved in presenting, and effectively handling high-stakes situations resides in what I have come to acknowledge as *mindset*. As a result, the topic of mindset is woven into all our engagements, regardless of the subject matter or whether the solution is designed for large groups, small groups, or individuals.

In our work, Sue and I have helped thousands of business professionals identify and understand the underlying mindsets that have held them back. There is nothing more fulfilling than witnessing our clients gain powerful insights about themselves and turn those insights into actions, allowing them to connect and lead with greater confidence. It is our hope that as you read *Deliberate Mindset*, you will begin this journey of self-discovery and change.

We believe having an empowered deliberate mindset is one of the biggest keys to living a life filled with success, connection, and happiness. We want to compel you to think about the way you think and challenge yourself to try new approaches.

How to Read Deliberate Mindset:

Over the years, we have read our fair share of personal growth and development books. It is the influence of these authors and thought leaders that has helped to shape our thinking, beliefs, and practices as coaches.

Our Disclaimer: While we are neither cognitive psychologists nor scientists, and our work is not a replacement for clinical psychological therapy, we are thrilled with the growing body of evidence around the subject of mindset. It verifies the consistent, empirical information we've experienced and noted with our clients over many years. Additionally, we've been very fortunate to know and collaborate with outstanding coaches and peers who share the same mindset about *mindset*. They have confirmed time and again: our approach is special, and it works.

We wanted to set a little context for you, before we dive in. Whether you are someone who likes to read books cover to cover, or you prefer to jump around based on specific interests, you can read this book in either way. To optimize your reading, we'd like to give you a quick glimpse of what you can expect to find in the pages of *Deliberate Mindset*. The first few chapters will take you through an exploration of what we mean by the term *mindset* and why we believe it can be learned, practiced, and mastered. Then, we'll introduce you to our Three-Step Process along with methods and techniques to put it into practice.

Three-Step Process:

1. Discover a mindset that isn't serving you. (We call this a **Default Mindset**.)

2. Make a choice to shift that default mindset. (We call this **Decide to Shift**.)

3. Create a new, more powerful mindset that can help you move beyond your current limitations and propel you to new levels of confidence, competence, and effective communication. (We call this creating a **Deliberate Mindset**.)

The final chapters focus on real-life situations that our coaching clients have faced. You will get a behind-the-scenes peek into how we helped clients uncover their default mindsets and the techniques we used to help them create more empowering deliberate mindsets. Along the way, we will point you toward stories that emphasize or elaborate on a specific technique. This way, if you prefer, you can jump to the section that is most relevant to you.

Finally, it is worth noting, this book is a product of our combined 40+ years of coaching experiences, observations, processes, and success stories with clients and colleagues. Because we've worked both together and independently with clients, sometimes we will use a collective voice, and other times we will be conveying our own individual stories and coaching experiences. Regardless of the voice we use or whose situations we are describing, our intention is for you to see yourself in some of these stories and that our ideas and tips for helping shift your mindset in high-stakes presentations and conversations will make a positive difference for you.

While reading, we encourage you to consider and explore how your mindset affects every relationship in your life. Not every technique or idea is going to resonate with you, and that's okay, but we request that you try them out before counting them out. We think you may be surprised by the results! If you're ready to take your personal and professional communication to the next level, let's begin.

CHAPTER 1

MAKING THE CASE FOR CONSIDERING MINDSET

As an expert in your field – an executive, senior manager, sales superstar, successful entrepreneur (or even if you are just getting started in your career), you have already succeeded on many levels to get where you are. To perform at the next level, your professional/technical competence is not going to be enough. On top of this foundation, you will need a new and more powerful combination of intellectual flexibility, emotional intelligence, and the ability to truly connect with people. As you progress further in your career, you will find (or have already found) that your technical competence matters less; it is just automatically presumed that you are technically competent. Personal presence and the ability to communicate about ideas and strategies (layered upon that foundation of technical competence) matter more.

When it comes to presenting and communicating, we all have blind spots that can undermine our ability to do our best. These hidden triggers can manifest as anxiety, fear, and discomfort – especially when faced with situations where the stakes are highest. We believe having a powerful mindset will ultimately drive our success. This type of emotional intelligence can be learned and nurtured with focus and attention. Having a well-prepared mindset – with the ability to quiet your mind and focus – ultimately has a much greater effect on your ability to succeed than white-knuckling your way through your fear and anxiety.

You know you're in a high-stakes situation when the consequences of winning or losing are personally or professionally serious. Consider the following:

> *Your PowerPoint deck is complete, and you have hours of preparation under your belt. Yet, walking into the client's office, you wonder if you have the moxie to pull it off. This is the first time a senior partner has turned over the bulk of the pitch to you, and you feel your nerves pumping. What if you stumble or freeze? What if your boss has to step in and take over, because you can't handle tough questions? You try to push these thoughts out of your mind as you begin with your opening remarks, but it is too late. Your mouth starts moving, but you have no idea what is coming out...*

How many times has insecurity or doubt clouded your mind before you even walked in the door? Even if you know your material and are successful in your field, how many times have you questioned yourself while presenting or thought to yourself, "Are they getting this? Do they like our approach? His body language seems resistant...what am I saying wrong?"

If these types of comments are running through your mind *while* you're having a conversation or presenting, how can you possibly be connecting and communicating with your listeners? We've all been there. None of the outcomes associated with being distracted by these thoughts are positive.

Change the Way You Think

Heightened emotions can derail the most seasoned professional when communicating in a high-stakes situation. The situations that trigger these emotions are different for everyone. Can you relate to any of the following situations?

- It is the first time you are leading a pitch to a potential client, and your firm's managing partner will be in the meeting with you.

- You are the youngest person at the table, and you are put on the spot to answer a question.

- You are one of the only females in a male-dominated industry/company.

- You have been asked to deliver a keynote speech to a group of 500 people.

- You need to deliver a project update to the management team, and the news is not going to be good.

- You must deliver difficult feedback to an employee who has a history of getting overly emotional.

- You have been asked to lead your company's new hire orientation meeting.

We would bet you have your own situations that have triggered negative emotions. The situation, itself, need not be business-related; it could be any conversation or public forum that is stressful for you. And let's face it, as you move through your career, more of these situations are going to arise, and you'll need more than technical competence alone to get you through.

In our years of working with business professionals, we know that tips and techniques designed to mask fear or nervousness can prevent us from connecting and being natural…mostly because they don't work. Masks often show up as quirky behaviors, such as:

- Being overly formal or overly familiar

- Moving too much or not enough

- Making strange hand gestures (i.e. clasping, behind back, in pockets)

- Sounding scripted or robotic

- Scanning the audience or pacing the room

- Experiencing dry mouth, shortness of breath, stuttering, and other issues.

To move beyond these types of derailing and potentially career-limiting behaviors requires a new and more powerful approach. The key is to employ a high degree of emotional intelligence, to connect with people, and to be natural.

The most significant change or breakthrough in a person's skills and confidence occurs when they think differently and create a complete shift in mindset – away from fear, trepidation, and masks, toward a place of certainty and expertise.

How can you learn to overcome these personal obstacles of growth to achieve your goals in life? To begin with, we believe it is critical to understand that communicating with credibility, impact, and influence is the most important skill for your future success. If you buy into this premise, the keys to getting there reside in your ability to both learn *and* master the mechanics of speaking *and* your mindset. We have seen novices and experienced professionals alike, increase their poise and polish by shifting or creating a new mindset.

Mechanics, Messaging and Mindset

While the purpose of this book is about the power of being able to shift and create a powerful mindset, we would be remiss if we didn't describe the other components that are critical parts of our coaching. In fact, many of the examples you will read throughout the following chapters illustrate the link that combines these components to help our clients create new mindsets. These are the three components:

MECHANICS

The mechanics of effective communication include: posture, movement, facial expression, gestures, pausing, voice tone, and eye contact. We spend a lot of time coaching and video recording clients to give them clarity about their strengths and weaknesses in these areas. Once mastered, these skills can make a huge difference in helping people feel more comfortable and contribute to their audiences perceiving them as confident and credible.

MESSAGING

While we can't help you create your technical content, we can help you structure your message in a way that gets attention quickly, provides clear calls to action, and gets to the point faster.

MINDSET

The key to managing your fears and helping you become comfortable, fully present, and agile in high-stakes situations resides in your ability to harness the power of your mindset to clear a path to your desired outcome.

Everyone agrees that knowing your content inside and out is critical, regardless of your audience, right? We coach our clients to master the mechanics of delivery and to learn how to craft effective messages which demonstrate their knowledge. But, as important as these two components are, it is mindset that ultimately affects presence and enables effective communication. We believe a powerful mindset is the underlying factor that determines success. Like any other skill, mastering it requires practice, coaching, and feedback.

What Makes the Stakes Higher?

In our experience, people struggle the most when there is a high-stakes element to a situation, presentation, or conversation. If you think back to childhood, an example of a high-stakes situation may have been reading aloud in front of your class...or maybe it was walking on stage to sing in the holiday concert (or *not* walking on stage at a holiday concert due to fear). From a very young age, we can all remember those feelings of anxiety, coupled with a deep desire to do well.

What high-stakes means is relative, of course, but anytime the outcome has great impact or value to you, we'd call that a high-stakes situation. Think about the range of emotions you feel when you are in a situation that is important to you. For example, you might experience a sense of anxiety as you eagerly await the green light on your project. Or you might feel a rush of adrenaline as you prepare to deliver a message you expect will produce a positive response from your audience.

Regardless of whether you are standing in front of a large conference, chairing a committee, or sitting across from a new client, you have *something* at stake. You are at risk personally. Your credibility and reputation can be enhanced or damaged as a result of your performance – no matter how mundane the topic of your presentation or conversation.

For those of you who present often, we are sure you can identify certain presentation situations that seem to have higher stakes than others. Perhaps you feel fear and anxiety conversing in front of a small group of highly technical experts who know twice as much about the topic as you do, or you might feel the screws tighten before you walk in to present to the board of directors.

We also know some people are energized by such situations. If that is the case, you are fortunate, and we want you to know you are in the minority. The majority of people do not share your enthusiasm. By far, the most common reaction among people we've worked with is one of fear.

Take a moment and reflect on a few presentations and conversations from your past and notice if any of them still trigger even a little bit of anxiety. Once you've gotten a few in mind, identify which ones seem to trigger angst or even fear.

As you reflect on these situations, can you identify whether you were trying to inform, persuade, or influence your audience? What we've found (and suspect you have too) is that the informational type of presentation or conversation holds the least amount of anxiety. If you are truly just informing a group, there is probably not a lot of risk involved for you personally, especially if the information was created by someone else and passed on to you to deliver without inserting your point of view. If the information contains bad news and is devoid of your point of view, you may be somewhat buffered from losing face, looking bad, or taking the blame. Your experience of this type of situation may trigger thoughts like the phrase we've all heard: "Hey, don't shoot me – I'm just the messenger."

However, if your presentation or conversation contains an influential component to it, it is very common for nerves to kick in. You are no longer just the messenger, so the stakes are higher. Presentations and conversations that require influencing or persuading are complex communications that can move whole groups of people, office staffs, boards of directors, etc., to alter their strategy, policies, procedures, or way of thinking.

If you are client-facing, chances are you will have to spend a lot of your time trying to influence people to buy your products or services. Remember, when you are only informing, you are devoid of a point of view. This isn't the case when you are attempting to persuade or influence. In this case, you'll most definitely want to express your point of view and gain acceptance or even enthusiasm from your audience.

The point of view might be that of your organization, you personally, or both. Either way, the moment you try to influence or sway an individual or group to a new way of thinking, the situation has a very different feel to it. By stating a point of view and requesting action from your audience that they are not currently taking, you are now opening yourself up to resistance, disagreement, criticism, disbelief, and many other unpleasant reactions.

When these moments occur, you'll want to be equipped with a confident mindset that will get you through the storm. Without such a mindset, it can be easy to fall into a downward spiral. These situations can tarnish your reputation and damage your credibility. The scary thing is that sometimes these downward spirals can pop up unexpectedly, and, without a deliberate mindset, you might suffer long-term effects.

Think about it. If you are new in the business world and fall into that downward spiral while talking with an important client, the consequences could haunt you for years. Even if you have significant experience and have done well in your career, a major snafu could destroy all the positive perceptions you have built over many years and end up negatively impacting your reputation.

Our recommendation is to examine the typical communication situations that feel bigger to you, the ones that matter, the ones where you feel that twinge in your gut. Have these in mind as you continue reading.

CHAPTER 2

YOUR MINDSET

We've already thrown around the term "mindset" many times, and while it might seem obvious what it means, we feel it would be helpful to provide our interpretation. According to Random House Dictionary, the first known use of the word "mindset" originated over 100 years ago in 1909, making it a virtual baby in the English language. For perspective, the word "attitude" was introduced in 1600s, "mental" dates to the 1400s, "emotional" from the late seventeenth century, and "feelings" from the 1100s. "Thought" came before the year 900, and "being" goes all the way back to 1275. "Paradigm," that new age buzzword, dates to 1480.

Words create our world, and some have been around much longer than we might have imagined. *Mindset* is a word whose definition is still being developed.

There are several dictionary definitions that are, at best, insufficient for our purposes:

- A mental attitude or inclination

- A fixed state of mind

- A tendency or habit.

These definitions hint at but don't really clarify what we mean. So, we created this definition:

Mindset: The lens through which we observe, perceive, create, and act.

Consider us your mindset optometrists. Throughout the rest of this book, we will ask you to look through different lenses to check your vision for the one that works best for you and the situations you face. The key to getting the most out of this work is to recognize that you always have options when considering what to do or how you think about a person or situation. This book provides ideas and tools to exercise those options when you need them.

Default Mindset

If you buy into the idea that your mindset affects what and how you perceive, thereby impacting your behavior and ability to communicate with ease and confidence in high-stakes situations, we ask you to consider that not all mindsets are created equal. Let's take the idea of mindset a step further. We want to introduce you to the *default mindset.* Consider the following example:

When David needs good-looking marketing pieces printed, he always goes to see his buddy, Joe. Joe's shop is five minutes from David's office; he does a great job; and he always meets his very tight deadlines – which are mostly the result of David's procrastination.

David vividly remembers the first time he walked into Joe's shop. The smell just about knocked him out! The chemical smell was so strong that he was sure brain tumors were beginning to grow. He couldn't help but wonder what could be happening to Joe and his staff as they breathed that seemingly toxic air every day.

After telling Joe what he needed, David asked him how he could deal with that terrible smell all day long. Joe's response was, "What smell?" He was serious, too. David was stunned that Joe could no longer recognize the smell. He had become desensitized to it, unaware of the strong smell of chemicals.

How many of you can relate to the "what smell?" remark Joe made? What is **your** version of "what smell?" Are you unconscious of something that could be detrimental to your success? Just as Joe was blind to the smell of the chemicals, we would assert that we all have long-term mindsets to which we are blind. We call these our default mindsets.

Default mindsets often live in our unconscious mind. Default mindsets are derived from the past, sometimes the long-ago past, and often are not distinguished as a mindset or anything else. They live like the truth within us. As we grow older, some of our earlier experiences affect our ability to withstand pressure or deal with change or failure. These default mindsets can develop early in our lives. For example:

A fifth-grade teacher says to a young student who is struggling with fractions, "Some people are just not cut out for math." In that moment, and with no intention to do so, the student decides she is inept at numbers and will direct all her future efforts to avoid dealing with them, in school or anywhere else. Her potential career as a CPA was nipped in the bud because she created an unconscious default mindset that said, "I'm not cut out for math." This mindset influenced her life in untold negative ways. She used that default mindset (or you could say the default mindset used her) in every decision she ever made about money, finance, and budgeting. For years, she never even kept score when she played golf.

Default mindsets are developed through the many experiences of our lives, mostly when we are young. Trying out for a play and not making it, getting bullied on the playground, and giving your first recital in grade school and freezing in front of the class are all examples. As young people, we make unconscious decisions about how to protect ourselves from experiencing these types of embarrassing or humiliating situations ever again. These decisions will often manifest later in life in the form of shying away from anything that feels risky or dangerous.

The default mindsets that are born out of these experiences will vary, of course, and we are not suggesting that every embarrassing or difficult moment in our lives limits us in high-stakes situations later. However, we have heard countless examples from our clients that link long-held and limiting default mindsets back to these types of situations.

We suspect there are as many examples of situations as there are people on the planet. The goal of this book is not to unravel your childhood, but we do want you to replace your default mindsets with new, more powerful mindsets that will serve you better.

Deliberate Mindset

A deliberate mindset is one that you consciously create. Your ability to think differently and shift away from a default mindset that isn't serving you can be a critical leverage point in just about any situation. Just as adrenaline can cause immediate increases in strength and speed in moments of crisis, a deliberate mindset can free you when you are confronted with any situation that causes dread, fear, or discomfort. Consider the following potential situations:

- You have been asked to be the keynote speaker at an upcoming conference.

- You need to request more resources for a highly visible and already expensive project.

- You are up for a promotion to partner in your firm, and you need to present your value proposition to the board.

- You are responsible for a huge change management initiative, and you need to personally generate buy-in from a resistant group of key stakeholders.

Every single time you enter these conversations, all cylinders better be firing. Creating and integrating a powerful, deliberate mindset will be key.

Given you are reading a book that falls within the genre of professional and personal development, we'll assume you may have created deliberate mindsets in the past, and you've had positive outcomes as a result. Think about the times when you had an internal dialogue before you started a presentation. It may have sounded something like, "Don't worry, I've got this. I'm prepared and ready for anything they can throw at me." Or maybe while coaching your kid's softball team, you found yourself helping the team shift their mindset at a critical point in the game.

There is tremendous power in being able to uncover a default mindset that might be undermining your confidence and then being able to replace it with a deliberate, more positive mindset. There is no magic involved in doing this, only the ability to make yourself aware of your mindset at any time. The process isn't difficult, but it takes conscious effort to develop the skills and build the mental muscle required to make it work. We promise that if you will do the work suggested, you will be able to create deliberate mindsets to support the outcomes you intend to produce.

Up to this point, we've been laying the foundation for a common understanding of what we mean by mindset and the importance of learning how to take conscious control over it. In theory, this probably makes sense. But what if you have a blind spot concerning a default mindset? How do you go about uncovering that blind spot? Then, when you discover a default mindset that isn't serving you, does that mean you are ready to do something about it?

The following sections will help you harness the power of intent and conscious awareness. Being able to do this will allow you to create a deliberate mindset that will set you up for success in high-stakes situations. In the upcoming pages, we will walk you through a three-step process to help you move from blind spots to results.

Three-Step Process:

- **DISCOVER YOUR DEFAULT MINDSET**
  Dig in and discover old, negative default mindsets that are hindering your progress and understand their impact on your ability to be successful in high-stakes situations.

- **DECIDE TO SHIFT YOUR MINDSET**
  Understand the importance of making a choice or declaration and choose to shift toward a new and deliberate mindset – one that will set you up for success.

- **CREATE A DELIBERATE MINDSET**
  Learn how to create and maintain a new, positive, and powerful deliberate mindset.

CHAPTER 3

STEP 1 - DISCOVER YOUR DEFAULT MINDSET

We believe human beings only take action for one of two reasons: avoiding pain or moving toward something pleasurable. Think about it. How many people do you know who clearly need help, a change, or even an intervention, and they don't see it themselves, but everyone else can? They are just not able to see what others see until something happens (often when the pain becomes overwhelming which spurs a shift in focus that ultimately springs them into action). Think of a relative or dear friend who is over-worked and stressed out. In addition to that, the doctor has told this person his/her blood pressure and cholesterol readings are way too high, and BMI is in the obese range. Outsiders can see very clearly this is a recipe for disaster, but no one can inspire your loved one to make any sustainable changes in diet, exercise, or reducing his/her workload. Then something happens...a heart attack, bad news, or the sudden loss of a job, and your friend finally has experienced enough pain to do something. Although we bring up this extreme situation, we don't want you to feel like you must go to the depths of despair before convincing yourself that creating a powerful, deliberate mindset can make a difference for you. We want you to be inspired by the possibility of the pleasure you will gain by being able to master your mindset.

The first step is uncovering possible default mindsets that might be influencing you. If you are in a place right now where you are trying to figure out what that blind spot might be, we encourage you to trust in the process and keep looking. This first step of uncovering a default mindset that isn't serving you can be one of the most difficult parts of the process. Yet, if you are open to the possibility that a default mindset is holding you back, we know you will find it extremely beneficial to uncover and deal with it.

Not all default mindsets are bad. For example, when Sue was growing up, her dad used to tell her that she could do anything she put her mind to. This instilled a very positive default mindset for Sue, such that whenever she approaches new things, she has an inner confidence that she will be able to figure it out.

All of us can conjure up positive default mindsets that have formed over the course of our lives. Unfortunately, when considering high-stakes situations, we would bet that most of us have developed some default mindsets that aren't serving us. When someone is struggling with a greater degree of nervousness or less confidence than usual, this is the first place to look.

It is our hope that by recognizing default mindsets that aren't serving you, you will be on your way to creating new mindsets that will be more empowering. If you struggle to uncover them, ask people you trust who are willing to tell you about blind spots they think you may have. In our work, we ask people a variety of questions to help them discover their default mindsets. Choose one of the following techniques to help you discover a potentially derailing default mindset for yourself:

- Examine Your Complaints

- Listen to Feedback

- Reflect

- Identify Grudges

Examine Your Complaints

The issues you most complain about are likely linked to a default mindset. Can you relate to some of these examples?

> *"My boss will never stop micromanaging me."*

> *"How many times do I have to ask for support?"*

> *"If the situation comes up again, I'm not going to say a word!"*

> *"There she goes again being hypercritical of every single thing I do. I can't do anything to please her!"*

Perhaps you've had similar complaints and are thinking, "How could a reaction to being micromanaged be linked to a default mindset?" It might not be, but the clues lie within the frequency of the complaint. If you feel micromanaged by every boss or person of authority with whom you've ever worked, that certainly could be an indicator of an area to pay attention to. It might be time to reflect and determine if this is a recurring theme and figure out where it originated. Constant complaints (the things your friends and family are sick of hearing you talk about!) are often rife with default mindset fodder.

How do negative default mindsets affect your ability to be confident in high-stakes situations? Let's take one from above and see how it plays out.

> *"There she goes again being hypercritical of every single thing I do. I can't do anything to please her!"*

If the person in this example is your boss, and you need to deliver a project status update to her that includes some bad news, this could trigger a default mindset and potentially derail you. Where did this default mindset come from? Is your boss hypercritical, or are you hypersensitive to objective feedback? These are the type of questions we would ask if you were working with us. You might discover that ANY critical feedback seems to sting, based on experiences you had growing up. Perhaps a teacher or parent had high standards for you, because they saw untapped potential. However, they weren't particularly good at acknowledging when you were doing well and, as a result, weren't able to inspire you to do better. It isn't hard to imagine how this early experience could have created a default mindset that caused you to interpret people of authority as hypercritical and out to get you. As we hinted earlier, your ability to recognize the trigger of a default mindset's creation is a critical first step in the process.

Listen to Feedback

Have you ever received feedback about a behavior that needs to change? That behavior may be linked to a default mindset. We suggest you listen carefully to the feedback. For example, you get consistent feedback that you appear too eager, and you're not really sure what it means. Upon reflection, you remember you have always tried extra hard to please people and make sure they like you. You didn't realize your attempts to please others came across as being overzealous or, perhaps, too eager.

You might be thinking, "How could coming across as too eager manifest negatively in a high-stakes presentation?" Consider that with this default mindset in place, you could be perceived as inauthentic, or you might assume a personal relationship too quickly. Additionally, there is the possibility you may be so consumed with being liked by the prospective client that you don't prepare as much as you could or should.

Reflect

There is great power in reflection in order to gain insights about yourself and situations that aren't working. The problem for most of us is that we don't take time to do it! When it comes to uncovering a default mindset that isn't serving you, take time to reflect on your high-stakes situations to find clues about beliefs or thought patterns that might be self-limiting. Consider the following background about Karen:

Karen was on the cusp of being promoted to director but needed help developing stronger relationships with clients. She also needed to generate new business, and all the partners in the firm told her she needed to be more assertive, especially in high-stakes, client-facing presentations and conversations.

Karen was very analytical and often too serious. Her approach was to jump right in and get down to business. She was not good at navigating conversations at the beginning of client meetings and expressed frustration that her peers seemed to naturally weave in and out of personal topics while effortlessly promoting their accomplishments. Her boss's perception was that Karen's demeanor made it awkward for clients.

In a situation like this, having a high degree of self-awareness is a must before anyone can start making real progress. We provide our clients with a variety of tools in order to gain perspective on how they analyze and approach situations, think, and relate to people. We find out what energizes them, identify where they shine, and help them identify their weaknesses. With Karen, it came to the surface quickly; one of her top strengths was humility.

People often get in trouble when they overuse a strength. For someone who is supposed to be making small talk to establish rapport with new acquaintances and provide a little personal disclosure to build relationships, humility was not the best attribute for Karen to leverage.

We discussed the fact that this strength was actually a *gift* to this organization, especially in the hard-driving type of culture she was in. Humility was something we didn't want Karen to lose, yet we wanted her to discover a new perspective on it and use it to her advantage.

I asked Karen to reflect on how this trait of humility had manifested itself throughout her life, and how it was helpful. She grew up as an only child of a single mother and believed that she needed to step up to the plate and keep her complaints to a minimum. She was naturally shy, extremely tall, and had been full-grown since the age of twelve. Suffice to say that Karen really didn't want to be seen. She preferred being in the background, avoiding being the focus of attention, and certainly didn't want the spotlight. Her saving grace was sports, where she channeled her natural competitiveness by being on a team instead of going solo.

One of the things we talked about early on was this belief that she held from childhood; was it possible this belief could change? Was that belief true, or was it something that she thought to be true based on life experience? She really had to challenge herself to look at successful people in the organization and realize her humility was not serving her well.

Karen used reflection to uncover a default mindset about humility that wasn't serving her. Our coaching engagement focused on helping her marshal this strength when it was warranted and diminish its power when she needed to step up to the plate.

Reflection can be an insightful process to help uncover a default mindset. Take time to reflect on past situations with the intention of uncovering beliefs that might still be derailing you in high-stakes situations.

Identify Grudges

Default mindsets can also take on the form of grudges. Grudges start small. Someone forgot to send a check, and we turned it into something more sinister. A spouse forgets an anniversary or a birthday, and a seed is planted. It doesn't take much to get a grudge started, but it can take a lifetime to melt away. We can only resolve a grudge if we actually choose to. It can happen in a moment, but only if we are aware that it exists.

If you identify that an old grudge is getting in the way of you being able to connect with your boss, you have succeeded in identifying a possible barrier within a default mindset that could hinder your ability to connect with her in high-stakes situations.

FINAL THOUGHTS ON IDENTIFYING A DEFAULT MINDSET

Identifying a default mindset involves reflection and the ability to uncover blind spots. We don't often take time to do this, and without a coach to prompt you, the responsibility lies with you. We strongly encourage you to pause, reflect, and think about situations or behaviors you want to improve. Look carefully and consider the possibility that the solution may be to change or shift out of a default mindset you've developed unintentionally, over time.

CHAPTER 4

STEP 2 - DECIDE TO SHIFT YOUR MINDSET

Once you've become conscious of a default mindset, you need to make a choice to do something about it. In our experience, it is helpful to declare to yourself (and others) that you will determine a different or new course of action. Let's face it: Simply becoming aware doesn't lead to a new result. If you know that your golf swing needs work, but you don't commit to going to the driving range and working with a golf coach on a regular basis, then your game will most likely continue as it always has.

Think about a New Year's resolution to lose weight. For most of the population, it's common knowledge that to lose weight, you need to eat healthier and exercise. Change isn't easy. Until a new habit or behavior becomes unconscious, it doesn't feel natural or integrated into our repertoire or style. It takes commitment, practice, and at times, some course correction. This step in the process, while seemingly simple, involves making a declaration or commitment to do the work. Here are some ideas that might help:

- Find an Accountability Partner

- Envision a Future State

- Write It Down

Find an Accountability Partner

To help ensure success, sometimes we need an outside influence to nudge or push us to go the extra mile. Just like having a workout buddy for exercise, find an accountability partner and have that person be your "mindset buddy." When you make a declaration to someone else that you are going to quit smoking or begin an exercise program, the stakes become higher for you as you're now accountable to another person. Similarly, declaring to someone that you are ready to let go of a negative, self-defeating mindset can reap the same benefits.

By virtue of the coaching process and agreements, the coach becomes the accountability partner. Typically, our process includes having regularly scheduled meetings. There are also actions and homework for which the coachee is accountable to complete between sessions, and when needed, we, as coaches and accountability partners, provide feedback along the way. Why not find someone to play that role for you? Seek out a close friend, relative, or colleague at work who is willing to hold you to your commitment to shift out of a negative default mindset. If you are serious about reaching your goals, you must find the right person. Following is a list of desirable characteristics we suggest you look for:

- **Ability to Be Objective:** Your accountability partner needs to be able to have an objective view of you and your situation or circumstances. Even if this person is a friend, you need to be explicit in your request. You might say something like: "Even though you might have a desire to side with me, I am asking that you provide an objective view of the situation. I may have a tendency to backslide into my old mindset, so I'll need your help in becoming aware of that and holding me accountable to my intentions."

- **Provides Honest Feedback:** You need someone to give you feedback along the way and not sugarcoat it. Give them permission to be brutally honest with you! You might say something like: "I need you to give it to me straight and not hold back. I may not like it, but I need to hear it."

- **Holds You Accountable:** This person needs to be willing to hold you accountable for what you say you're going to do. If you tell this person that you are committed to stopping negative self-talk, and they hear you start to go down the rabbit hole, they need to be willing and able to call you on it. And equally as important, you need to be willing to listen!

Envision a Future State

Whether it's losing weight or delivering a stellar presentation, it is critical for you to envision what success looks like. As the name of this technique describes, you want to create a mental image of what that future state looks and feels like. The scientific evidence about the brain and its ability to respond to visualization is abundant and has been used predominantly with athletes for decades.

Research by Srinivasan Pillay, a Harvard educated M.D. and author of *Your Brain and Business: The Neuroscience of Great Leaders*[1], explains how visualization works:

"We stimulate the same brain regions when we visualize an action as we do when we actually perform that same action." says Pillay.

According to his research using brain imagery, visualization works because neurons in our brains (those electrically excitable cells that transmit information) interpret imagery as equivalent to a real-life action. When we visualize an act, the brain generates an impulse that tells our neurons to perform the movement. This creates a new neural pathway – clusters of cells in our brain that work together to create memories or learned behaviors – that primes our body to act in a way consistent to what we imagined. All of this occurs without actually performing the physical activity, yet it achieves a similar result.

How Does Visualizing Your Desired Outcome Help You Decide and Declare to Shift Your Mindset?

If you are aware of a negative default mindset that is triggering you as you prepare for a high-stakes presentation to the executive leadership team, you need to be willing to do the work to shift it. Sometimes that work is quick and easy; other times it's not. You may need to spend several weeks or months developing the mental muscle required to change a pattern of thinking.

1.Srinivasan Pillay (Pearson Education, Inc. 2011)

It's not unlike the example of wanting to lose weight. For Sue, seeing pictures of herself before she had her twins created a positive image of a goal she wanted to attain. Seeing that image (when she was feeling discouraged or tired and didn't want to work out) helped her recommit to getting back to a healthy weight. This ultimately inspired her to go to the gym.

Do what works best for you. Some people create vision boards with pictures that inspire them. Others write a list of the positive outcomes that could be achieved once a plan is complete.

You could also ask yourself: "How do I want to be perceived in an upcoming meeting?" Envision yourself embodying all the characteristics required to be perceived that way. For example, back to that presentation to the executive leadership team, you might want to be perceived as competent, confident, and passionate. Can you envision what you would look and sound like if you embodied those characteristics? See yourself standing confidently in front of that team, effortlessly delivering your prepared content, and managing the questions in a conversational, competent manner.

The practice of envisioning yourself in the future helps you commit to the work required to shift a negative default mindset. The possibilities are endless.

Write It Down

People support what they create, and part of making that creation process tangible is writing it down. Whether you use a journal, notes on your smartphone, or simply enter a task in your calendar, documenting your commitments is powerful. You can take this technique to the next level by creating a visual queue that serves as a trigger to remind you of what you've committed to. It could be as simple as putting a post-it note on your mirror, so you see it every time you brush your teeth. Depending on the situation, it might be something as simple as: "Remember your commitment to yourself!" or "Spend time preparing your mindset, not just your PowerPoint deck!"

Additional tip: Share what you've written with your accountability partner. This puts even more "skin in the game" for you to follow through on your commitment.

The Power of Steps 1 & 2 in Practice

How "Discovering a Default Mindset" and "Deciding to Shift" paved the way for success:

Uncovering an Overly Competitive Style

William struggled with engaging and managing his remote team. He had a rapid-fire pace of communicating that lacked clarity. During conference calls, he would rarely pause to listen, check for understanding, or ask questions. Additionally, he didn't make time to have developmental conversations with the people who reported to him. He only talked to them when a project warranted an intervention, or updates were required. The result of all this was a team that had little clarity about roles and goals, and they weren't engaged in their projects at the necessary level. Although William had received feedback on all the above, he wasn't able to do anything about it – at least not anything sustainable. During an early coaching session, we uncovered a default mindset that was a blind spot for William – a strong competitive style of communication. I asked him to consider where this came from, and he related the following:

"When I was growing up, I had a brother who was thirteen months older than me, and we were in constant competition with each other. I was always trying to catch up to him, get better grades, have the answers sooner, and run faster – you name it! I was consumed with beating him and being right all the time. It's something that exists between us to this day!"

I asked him if he thought this competition with his brother had any effect on how he related to his team. A light bulb went on for William! (This is one of those delicious moments in coaching when the client connects the dots and can make a significant shift. As coaches, we can never get enough of these moments.)

He recognized for the first time that he was constantly competing for airtime with his team, and this manifested itself in how he communicated with them. He didn't want to ask them questions or pause to give them a chance to chime in, because he was consumed with being the one with all the answers…and not just the right answers, but also the first answers! He realized that because he didn't have anyone "looking out for him" early on in his career, he didn't see this as an important role he needed to take on as a manager of others. Once he recognized he had a default mindset around competing which affected how he related to his team, he was able to move onto the next step in the process – making a choice to create a new, deliberate mindset that would change the way he interacted with his team.

He recognized that being competitive with his brother served him while he was growing up and trying to succeed, but now it was hindering his ability to engage and motivate his team. He thought about the effect this had on specific people who reported to him and realized it was probably shutting them down.

Operating from his default mindset, he perceived that the people who reported to him weren't proactive enough, didn't speak up enough, or didn't do enough.

This realization gave him the motivation to do something different. He made a choice – a deliberate choice. He declared to himself, and to me, that he was ready to do something tangible about it. I was his accountability partner in the process. This was a pivotal moment for William, because he was now ready to get to work.

FINAL THOUGHTS ABOUT DECIDING TO SHIFT YOUR MINDSET

The moment you are motivated from within to do something different is the moment sustainable change can begin. Don't make the mistake of jumping into action too soon. Once you have discovered a negative default mindset, take the time to make the deliberate choice about what you are going to do about it and declare it. This step will set you up for success.

CHAPTER 5

STEP 3 - CREATE A DELIBERATE MINDSET

Now it's time for action. You've uncovered a default mindset, and you've made the choice and declared you will do something about it. Now you must determine the approaches and techniques that will help you create a deliberate, more powerful mindset. As energizing as this step may seem on the surface, it can feel unfamiliar and more challenging than expected when you are learning to do this; there is a process and learning curve involved.

Generating Competence

Have you ever learned to drive a car with a manual transmission? In the beginning, each push of the clutch and shift of the stick felt clunky and intentional. If you kept it up and practiced, chances are you were eventually able to drive a manual transmission car without even thinking about it. Do you remember the first time you tried a new sport? Perhaps you remember learning to play a musical instrument or the steps of a new dance. The process is the same in all circumstances in which you are building muscle memory and training your mind and body to work together. The key to mastering new skills and behaviors is practice, course correction (if needed), and repetition. Using this approach will get you to the place at which the new behavior or skill is fully integrated and feels natural. Some might say it flows.

You will go through a similar process as you learn how to identify and change your own mindset. The Four Levels of Competence Model[2] (figure 1) provides another way to understand this process. It is not clear who originated the very first 'conscious competence' learning model. Various modern authors, as well as

Figure 1

4 LEVELS OF COMPETENCE

UNCONSCIOUS COMPETENCE
The new habit, skill, or mindset becomes part of your natural delivery or way of doing things. You don't need to consciously think about it anymore. It's natural, and it flows.

UNCONSCIOUS COMPETENCE

④

CONSCIOUS COMPETENCE

CONSCIOUS COMPETENCE
You begin to apply a new process or skill but need to put a lot of focus on it to be successful. If you don't continue to practice and push through this stage, you will most likely slip back down to Conscious or Unconscious Incompetence.

CONSCIOUS INCOMPETENCE
You are made aware of the bad habit, skill, or mindset that isn't serving you.

CONSCIOUS INCOMPETENCE
(This is Where Behavior Change Can Begin!)

③

②

UNCONSCIOUS INCOMPETENCE
(You Start Here)

UNCONSCIOUS INCOMPETENCE
You are unaware of a bad habit, skill, or mindset that isn't serving you.

①

---

2. Found in *Human Performance and Productivity. Vol 2: Information Processing and Decision Making*, W C Howell and EA Fleishman (eds.), Erlbaum; 1982

sources as old as Confucius and Socrates are cited as possible earliest originators.

1. UNCONSCIOUS INCOMPETENCE

At the first level, you are **unaware** of a bad habit, approach, or default mindset that isn't serving you. Since you aren't even aware of it, there is nothing you can do about it. It is in your blind spot.

2. CONSCIOUS INCOMPETENCE

At the second level, you have become **aware** of the bad habit, approach, or mindset that isn't serving you. This is the point at which behavior change can begin. In our work, we spend considerable time video-recording our clients, so they can see what needs to change for them. We typically hear clients saying something like, "Wow, I had no idea I said 'um' 25 times in that short presentation. Now that I know I did, I can do something about it!" Recognition is only the first step. You need a plan of action and possibly coaching and feedback to start doing things differently to get to the next level. (This is a great place where your accountability partner can help you.)

3. CONSCIOUS COMPETENCE

At the third level, you've become very aware of your conscious incompetence. The next step is to practice and execute specific techniques that will lead you to conscious competence. Since we are dealing with breaking old habits, approaches, or default mindsets and replacing them with empowering ones, this is the most challenging level. It takes a significant amount of mental focus to successfully turn old habits into new behaviors. If you are getting coached or working diligently to change a behavior, your initial efforts may feel unnatural, awkward, or even clunky. Keep in mind, these uncomfortable feelings are normal at this stage; it is a natural part of the learning curve.

4. UNCONSCIOUS COMPETENCE

At the fourth level, you have created new habits, and it feels natural. You don't have to think about them anymore. When you figure out how to quickly recognize a default mindset that isn't serving you and shift into a deliberate mindset that is more powerful, you have reached a level of unconscious competence. It takes time and lots of practice to get to this level.

Our advice when coaching clients is to embrace and work through the awkward stages of getting to unconscious competence. The same holds true when changing the way you think in order to create a new, more powerful mindset.

Approaches to Create Deliberate Mindsets

Over the years, we have tried various approaches in our own lives and with the people we've coached. There isn't a one-size-fits-all solution. There will always be situations in which you need to shift your mindset. Some will require an immediate shift, and others will be longer term. Our goal is to help you build a sustainable mindset that will keep you grounded, prevent knee-jerk reactions, and help you perform your best in high-stakes situations.

Consider the following examples that may trigger you and require discipline to quickly shift your mindset, if you intend to produce a positive outcome:

- Someone derails your agenda during a presentation and asks an unexpected question.

- As you are giving feedback to an employee, the person begins to cry.

- You are cut off in traffic and have to quickly maneuver your car to avoid an accident.

- You are about to walk into a meeting with someone with whom you have ongoing tension.

When practiced over time, it is possible for you to get to a place where, in a very short period of time, you're able to shift from upset and fear to neutrality and calm.

The following techniques work and are applicable to any situation:

- Acknowledge Your Emotions

- Stop-Challenge-Choose

- Pause and Breathe

- 24-Hour Rule

- Find Another Way to Say It

- Pick a Mantra

- Laugh

- Meditate

- Point of View Model

- Create a Game

Acknowledge Your Emotions

We are about to share one of the best techniques to help you begin the process of creating a deliberate mindset. The key lies in your ability to acknowledge negative emotions you might be feeling in relation to the situation you are about to enter. If your emotional state is associated with a negative mindset, left unchecked, it could derail you. Reflect on those times when nerves kicked in as you were preparing for a presentation. How did this affect the outcome? Emotions associated with anxiety or nervousness strongly affect your ability to be effective. Ultimately, you know if you want to be perceived as competent, credible, and confident, and you are feeling anxious, you will *not* come across the way you intend.

These lower-grade emotions cause stress, and stress triggers the hormone, cortisol, which exacerbates the physiological symptoms associated with stress: tight stomach, sweating, heart racing, etc. Amy Cuddy, an American social psychologist at Harvard University, has done research on the impact of cortisol on stressful situations and how that relates to presence. She delivered one of the most-watched TED Talks in history, called, "Your Body Language Shapes Who You Are," in which she talks about how to create a higher degree of composure. Consider going to YouTube and watching her talk – we recommend it to our clients.

Take a serious look at your emotions and how they might link to a default mindset that isn't serving you. By first acknowledging the negative emotion and corresponding mindset, you'll be in a better position to choose a more positive one and, subsequently, go about the process of shifting it. Take a look at The Powerful Presenter's Mindset Scale below (Figure 2) and see if you can recall a previous situation when you were on the lower end of the scale. Equally as important, what was the impact of these emotions on your ability to deliver a powerful presentation?

How to Use "The Powerful Presenter's Mindset Scale"

The goal of The Powerful Presenter's Mindset Scale is to help you determine the gap between WHERE YOU ARE and WHERE YOU WANT TO BE. When we first created it, our intention was to provide a practical model to help our clients feel more empowered during their preparation for high-stakes presentations. The approach allows you to correlate your current emotional state with your current mindset. Doing so will give you a baseline from which to "move up" using one of the techniques outlined below. Our suggestions on how to use the model:

1. On the left side of the scale – identify the emotion you are feeling.

2. On the right side of the scale – identify the corresponding mindset that seems to resonate best with you.

3. If you ranked yourself lower on the scale than you want to be, choose one of the techniques on the following pages to help you shift upward.

Figure 2

The Powerful Presenter's Mindset Scale

Identify How You Feel

Identify Your Mindset

EMOTIONAL Scale		MINDSET Scale
CONFIDENT	1	DYNAMIC
CALM	2	FOCUSED
HOPEFUL	3	READY
NEUTRAL		
UNEASY	4	ROBOTIC
FEARFUL		
OVERWHELMED	5	SCATTERED

CLIMB UP ONE RUNG AT A TIME

EMOTIONAL Scale

MINDSET Scale

It is very rare that we find clients going from the bottom of the scale all the way to the top at once. We tell our clients to start climbing up one rung at a time and to be patient if they find that they aren't climbing upward as fast as they desire. The impact of intentionally shifting your emotional state from a negative to a more positive state will create a momentum that will have a very powerful impact on your overall mindset, even if it appears to be a minor shift.

Stop-Challenge-Choose

In our experience, the first and most important technique to cultivate is the ability to prevent your emotions/feelings from driving your reactions and responses when faced with high-stakes presentations and conversations. In order to get the results you are looking for, you need to be balanced and objective when choosing how to react. The Results Model[3], developed by Larry Wilson, (Figure 3), provides an easy roadmap to remember when you are being triggered:

1. **STOP** in the moment when you recognize you are being triggered by an **event** that is causing a negative reaction.

---

3. Found in *Play To Win! Choosing Growth Over Fear in Work and Life* - Larry Wilson and Hirsch Wilson (Bard Press, edition #2, 2004)

2. **CHALLENGE** your feelings or assumptions about the situation. NOTE: your feelings and assumptions about the event are largely driven by filters that come in the form of biases and/or a negative default mindset. These filters need to be challenged!

3. **CHOOSE** a mindset or reaction that will produce a more objective **external response**, giving you the result you are seeking.

Figure 3

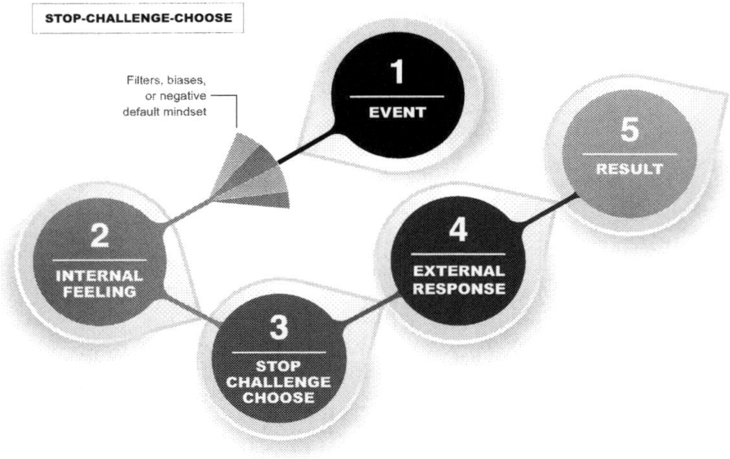

Using Stop-Challenge-Choose to Overcome the "Youngest Person in the Room Syndrome"

Katherine was a junior consultant at a professional services firm. Up to this point, she'd mainly been an independent contributor supporting senior partners and managing directors for the execution of client projects. She was told she needed to work on her presence and ability to persuade clients during meetings. At the onset of the coaching, she told us she thought what hindered her most was the perception that she was too young to be advising clients who could be her parents' age. "I just think that it's going to take a while for me to break through this perception. I know my stuff; I'm one of the smartest in my peer group. I don't think they want to listen to me, because I appear inexperienced and young." (A classic default mindset in action...) She had an underlying belief that she didn't have a right to be at the table because of her age. We set out to change that and started as we almost always do – we got her in front of the camera.

We recorded her. She watched the playback and was stunned. She stood with her legs and arms crossed the entire time. She had chronic up-speak (the phenomenon where the end of a sentence sounds like a question and has the impact of making people sound unsure, immature, and inexperienced). She also looked down a lot when she was thinking. Not to mention every other word was um, so, or ya know.

So, we got to work. We coached her on developing a more powerful, balanced stance. We repeatedly worked on helping her embrace silence and speak with punctuation in order to get rid of her of fillers and up-speak. We gave her techniques to connect better with her eye contact. She worked hard during our sessions and then in-between sessions to build the muscle memory required to get her to a stage of unconscious competence with the skills.

During one of our final sessions, she had the experience of seeing herself through a different lens on video playback. She was executing the skills and didn't appear inexperienced at all! She looked confident, articulated her thoughts in a concise and compelling manner, and looked people in the eye. It was a transformative experience for Katherine, but would her newfound confidence stick the next time she was asked to participate in a client meeting? As we've said many times so far, mastery of the delivery skills is only part of the equation. In order for Katherine to truly embody the confidence she needed, she had to come up with a way to STOP the negative internal dialogue feeding into her mindset.

Katherine reported that even though she was feeling more confident in the delivery skills, she still found herself having pangs of doubt and insecurity before walking into client meetings. The resulting impact was that she fell back into bad habits. As she described it, her self-conscious mindset impacted her ability to look people in the eye. She also noticed that her breathing became shallower and caused her to rush through her sentences and not to pause. And the senior partners were noticing... not good.

Katherine needed a way to halt the negative spiral before walking in the door, so we introduced her to the Stop-Challenge-Choose technique. We helped her to connect the dots between her negative default mindset and her ability to maintain composure in high-stakes client meetings.

Step 1: STOP the thoughts immediately. Once she recognized her increasing heart rate and self-defeating thoughts, she needed to turn them off.

Step 2: CHALLENGE the negative assumptions. It wasn't enough to just stop thinking negative thoughts; she needed to challenge the validity of those thoughts. She created a couple of mantras to help her do this. She would say to herself, "I don't need to buy into that – I am prepared, the senior partner believes in my value, and I have earned the right to be here."

Step 3: CHOOSE a response to help achieve the desired outcome. In Katherine's case of wanting to be perceived as confident and competent, she needed to replace the self-limiting thoughts with more empowering behaviors and beliefs. She made a conscious choice to focus her attention on her client rather than on herself which then allowed her to be more conversational and present to what was going on in the room.

Katherine's homework was to employ this technique before her next client meeting. During our final coaching session, she reported a new sense of calm that she had never experienced. She told us the following:

"Based on the success I experienced with all the other skills we worked on, I trusted the Stop-Challenge-Choose *technique would work too…I just had no idea how powerful it was. I was about to go into a meeting where I needed to present some competitive intelligence to our client. I started to feel the rumblings of doubt about two hours before the meeting, so I immediately stopped myself cold. Actually, that was the hardest part; because*

I had become so used to feeding into my negative mindset — the internal dialogue was pretty loud! I shifted away from that old mindset and challenged it with what I knew to be true: I was prepared, and the research was sound and backed up by the senior partner on the account. I found myself repeating this cycle a few times before we walked in the door, and I even shared the technique with my boss! Right as we were walking into the meeting, I focused my attention on our client, who was eager to hear our results. What we had to tell him was a critical piece of the strategy they were about to implement, so I felt like we were truly partnering with the client to make a difference. It was great. And the best news was that my boss was blown away. On the taxi ride back to the office, he went on and on about what a striking difference he had seen in me. Definitely one of the highlights of my career so far!"

Pause and Breathe

During the *Stop* phase above, we strongly suggest that you pause and breathe for a moment. Yes, just breathe. We are sure you have heard this before; it's not revolutionary. Yet many of us forget the power of breathing. Deep breathing. When you breathe deeply, it sends a message to your brain to calm down and relax. The brain then sends this message to your body. Those things that happen when you are stressed, such as increased heart rate, increased cortisol (the stress hormone), and fast breathing, all decrease as you breathe deeply to relax.

Next time you feel your current mindset may hinder your ability to have an even-keeled conversation, take the time to *breathe*. You will perform better. Breathe deeply before the interaction and then occasionally while in the midst of it.

FOUR COUNT BREATHING TECHNIQUE

Breathe in for four counts, hold your breath in for four counts, breathe out for four counts, and then hold for four counts. Repeat several times. IMPACT: Focuses your attention away from nerves AND has the calming effect of lowering cortisol and decreasing the heart rate.

24-Hour Rule

If you've tried to stop and breathe (or perhaps used the four-count breathing technique) and it hasn't worked, you need more time to step back and disconnect from the situation. If it is a high-stakes situation, and you have the opportunity to buy yourself time before engaging or making a decision, we suggest waiting 24 hours before you do so. Many of us can remember our parents telling us to "Sleep on it. You will feel better in the morning." This isn't any different! We've all had situations where we have gotten triggered for some reason and engaged in a conversation with a whole bunch of adrenaline feeding into a negative mindset. This is just a friendly reminder to heed our parents' advice and take a step back for 24 hours to gain perspective. Using the 24-hour buffer can help you think more clearly to make better decisions.

Find Another Way to Say It

How many times have you found yourself venting or complaining about a situation and (by the end of your rant) not feeling better but rather more amped up and frustrated? That's the issue with focusing on the problem and talking about it incessantly to anyone who will listen – it only keeps it alive and often amplifies its energy.

We have a technique you can use when you get the urge to complain or feed into a negative aspect of an issue. It's called *Find Another Way to Say It*. Here's how it works.

Say you are about to go into a meeting with a cross-functional team, and the senior member of the finance department will be attending. He has always proven to shut down the brainstorming and ideas and generally has a negative disposition toward many projects. Whether you are venting to yourself or to a friend, for every negative thing you say, try to *Find Another Way to Say It*.

For example, if you typically say something like:

> *"Great…another meeting with John – he's such a jerk. He's going to derail the agenda, like he always does, right in front of our CFO. And of course, it's on ME to keep us on track. How am I going to keep the agenda moving forward without him hijacking it?"*

Say to yourself or anyone you are talking to, "I can find another way to say this!"

> *"Okay, here goes...another meeting with John...at least I know what to expect...and I know I can't control him."*

Say to yourself again, "I can find an even *better* way to say this!"

> *"Let's try this again...another meeting with John...I expect he will try to shoot down my ideas. My challenge today will be to have him engage in a discussion about how we can make a new idea work rather than just dismiss it."*

You get the point. When it comes to setting ourselves up for success, often the conversations we have in our heads predetermine what the outcomes will be. This is so important, we want to say it again: **Often the conversations we have in our heads predetermine what the outcomes will be.**

Whether you relieve stress by venting to co-workers, or you just have a nasty internal dialogue about something, our strong suggestion would be to find another way to say it next time and see what happens to your mindset. Our experience is that it will improve exponentially when you shift what you are saying to yourself and *Find Another Way to Say It!*

Pick a Mantra

You may not call it a mantra, but many people have sayings or phrases they live by or that come to mind when the going gets tough. We recognize sayings such as, "Do something that scares you every day." (Eleanor Roosevelt) or "When life gives you lemons, make lemonade!" As cheesy as some of them may sound, we are not surprised when our clients quote one of these phrases as a mantra of sorts that keeps them moving ahead despite what is being thrown their way. Go online and Google famous quotes by people you admire. Think of a quick phrase or saying that can get you unhooked quickly if you feel yourself drifting into a negative spiral before a high-stakes situation. Here are some of our favorites. Feel free to use them!

- Everything is temporary.

- You never regret doing the right thing.

- How will I feel about this a week from now? A month from now? A year from now?

- What's the worst that can happen?

- I'm prepared and ready – it's time to just go for it!

- I've got this.

- We're not curing a terminal illness here!

- I have earned the right to be at the table.

Create your own mantras that you can use to help soothe fear, anxiety, or nerves before or during high-stakes situations. Consider our friend Pat's story. The outcome generated a mantra he uses to this day!

Find the Booger

Pat was asked to meet with the governor of his state because he wanted Pat to participate in a lawsuit for a cause near to the governor's heart. While Pat was passionate about the cause and eager to get involved at a deeper level, he was also aware of the anxiety he was feeling merely at the thought of meeting someone with the level of notoriety and authority like the governor.

Pat was feeling a combination of emotions – excitement, curiosity, honor, nervousness, and anxiety. He knew that he had to get a grip on these conflicting emotions before he walked into the governor's office, but he was at a loss about how to do that. He decided to just show up and try to remain composed.

He arrived at the governor's office and sat in his waiting room, sweating with nervous anticipation. He didn't want to embarrass himself. During his long wait, his anxiety mounted with each passing minute. Eventually, he was led into an office and was motioned to sit on a sofa at the other side of the room. He was now physically trembling. The governor finally got off the phone and began walking toward him, as Pat quivered. The governor greeted him warmly; Pat smiled and said his greetings quite confidently. Beginning with a little small talk, Pat felt the last of his nerves fade away, as he was able to focus only on the giant booger that hung from the governor's nose. The governor was human...he had boogers.

In his encounter with the governor, Pat was lucky that a personal hygiene issue gave him some freedom. By accident or not, he was never seriously intimidated by a person of power again. From that point forward, whenever Pat was in a situation where he felt intimidated by a person who he felt had power, he used this mantra: "They are human...they have boogers." This mantra gave him access to a new deliberate mindset that has served him well.

We all have those moments when we need something to interrupt our thinking and remind us that we are okay, and whatever happens, we will be okay. Often the very act of using a mantra will clear the space for you to be more successful. Pick one and stick it on the wall where you can see it.

Laugh

"The sound of roaring laughter is far more contagious than any cough, sniffle, or sneeze."[4] Laughter is proven to help your brain release the feel-good neurotransmitters: dopamine, serotonin, and an array of endorphins. Therefore, it should come as no surprise that by inducing laughter, you will set yourself up for a much more positive mindset.

> *"Your sense of humor is one of the most powerful tools you have to make certain that your daily mood and emotional state support good health."[5]*

---

4. Cited: *Laughter is the Best Medicine* 4/25/13 Paul McGhee on JB Bonds.com

5. Paul E. McGhee, Ph.D., Pioneer in Humor Research and Creator of The Laughter Remedy

For example, Jeff regularly uses this technique when he is in his car and needs to shift his mindset before going to an important meeting. He will either call his friend, Marcus, or listen to two voicemails he has saved on his phone from him that are particularly funny. Whenever he needs a mindset shift or wants to intentionally laugh, he listens to these voicemails. Likewise, Sue will call her brother, Dan, when she needs comic relief. Ironically, she too has a couple of particularly funny voicemails she has saved from him that induce instant laughter when she listens!

Here are some other ways to generate laughter:

- Watch your favorite TV show or clips of funny excerpts on YouTube. Sue loves to watch clips from The Office (American OR British version) whenever she wants to laugh.

- Call a friend who can make you laugh. Tell them, "I need to laugh right now – what do you have for me?"

- Intentionally remember a funny story or event that always makes you laugh.

Laughter is not only good for shifting your mindset in the moment, but it helps you remember not to take life or yourself too seriously. Having a few go-to's in the laughter department can really help you shift your mindset in a pinch!

Meditate

The practice of meditation has gone from being a hippy, fringe movement to a mainstream health practice. There is mounting evidence that proves the benefits of meditation for mind, body, behavior, and relationships. The National Institute of Health has invested $24 million in research to show the connection between meditation and improved health conditions, including reduced risk factors for hypertension, diabetes, and obesity; increased lifespan; reduced thickening of coronary arteries; reduced blood pressure in comparison with other procedures; reduced heart failure; and reduced use of hypertension medication. Even *Time Magazine* published a special edition in 2017 entitled: *Mindfulness*.

Our intention isn't to take a deep dive into all the research, but to provide specific evidence that proves the benefits of meditation. We want to focus on why we think meditation can have a long-term effect on your ability to shift your mindset in high-stakes situations. It works, and here are a few ideas on how to get started.

Meditation in the Moment

> *When Sarah was on conference calls with her team, she needed something to remind her to pause more, ask more questions, and let them come up with answers on their own. Her determination was so strong, she decided she needed to do something to shift her mindset before each call. When I suggested meditation, she resisted, saying, "I don't have time to do that…and how would meditating help me? I just need to learn to shut my*

mouth!" I knew I couldn't force her to try it, and she would have to experience the positive impact of quieting her mind on her own. One might say she had a default mindset about meditation, but that's another story! I suggested rather than feeling as if she needed to go into a deep meditative state, perhaps she could push back her chair for five minutes before the call, shut her eyes, and just breathe and relax. I told her to trust in the process and just try it a couple of times.

I wasn't surprised that on our next call two weeks later, Sarah had positive things to report about this new practice. Not only did it give her time to transition from the work she was doing prior to the call and to clear her mind, but she also reported being calmer and more patient as a result. The proof for her was the new level of engagement she was seeing in her team on calls. It was enough evidence for her to keep doing it!

Start Small

Meditation doesn't have to be ominous; you don't have to hole yourself up for hours a day in silence. It can be integrated into your everyday life, and you can receive the amazing benefits of being able to quiet your mind on a regular basis. It could be as simple as closing your eyes for ten minutes and focusing on your breath. In our coaching engagements, we often teach meditation to our clients as a pathway to relieve stress and become more grounded. Many of our clients express intimidation at the thought of meditating. We often hear comments like, "I can't ever quiet my mind, and if I have to do that for five minutes, I'm more stressed out!" or "I don't have time to meditate." We get it. Meditation is a practice that not only takes time to do, but it also takes focus and repetition to hone your ability to quiet your mind.

Try These Ideas

- Schedule a ten-minute break in your calendar every day. Choose a time you won't be interrupted, perhaps at the beginning of your day or during lunch. Shut your door or find a quiet space. Then set the timer on your phone, close your eyes, and just breathe. Don't judge any thoughts that float into your mind, just go back to focusing on your breath. The benefits will be rejuvenated thinking, a clear mind, and energy to put toward the rest of your day.

- Set your alarm ten minutes early in the morning and lie in bed; feel the comfort of your bed, your pillow, and the blankets that surround you. Bask in the comfort you feel and breathe deeply.

- Use an application on your smartphone to assist you. Here are some of our favorites:

  1. **Buddhify** – great for people on the go. You can listen to short guided meditations when you're at the airport, waiting in line, between meetings, or if you're feeling stressed out.

  2. **Headspace** – created by a trained Tibetan Buddhist monk, Headspace provides a free 10-day trial and only takes 10 minutes per day!

3. **Whil.** – created by the founders of lululemon, this app allows you to relax and power down your mind with traditional guided meditation practices and video yoga sessions. Don't have time to decide which practice you want? You can input your mood, intention, and, amount of time you have, and the app combs through its database and identifies the most fitting option.

4. **Insight Timer** – for a more seasoned meditator, this app lets you choose preferred interval time, ending bell sound, and ambient noise. You can also see in real time who else in the Insight Timer community around the world is meditating!

While the benefits of meditation are clear, our experience in our own lives and those of our clients is that it makes a huge difference in one's ability to access a more positive and empowering mindset. Additionally, the benefits of this technique are cumulative. Just like working out at the gym, the more consistently you go, the greater results you will get. You can't simply go to the gym and take a cycling class two days before vacation and expect to have a beach body! Meditation works the same way. While you will feel immediate benefits like a quieter mind, more peacefulness, and energy, the best results occur over time.

Point of View Model

If you are open to the realization that your truth is not the only truth, then we'll assume you've accepted the idea that other viewpoints could be valid. Further, are you willing to consider that other viewpoints are not only valid but could possibly be even more legitimate than yours? Whoa – how about that!

We have created a simple model that will help you consider other people's points of view (Figure 4). By using this model in the manner we recommend, a mindset shift may come easily to you. For others, the process may be more challenging. The good news is it's possible to make this shift, as long as you can remain open to it. Consider the following story from a coaching engagement Sue was involved with.

Figure 4

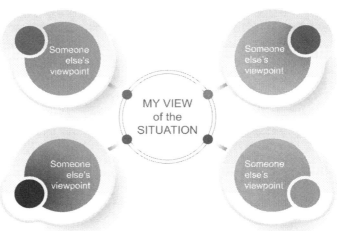

POINT OF VIEW MODEL

Someone else's viewpoint

Someone else's viewpoint

MY VIEW of the SITUATION

Someone else's viewpoint

Someone else's viewpoint

Jumping to Conclusions

Toward the end of a year-long coaching engagement, Steve found himself in a dilemma. It was performance review time, and his bonus was linked to the outcome.

Shortly after the reviews were complete, Steve's boss, Rajit, transitioned into a leadership role in the company. Steve was eagerly waiting to hear feedback about his performance and bonus. He'd had a rough year. Not only had he been working on some challenging communication issues (hence the coaching), he also was coping with a lot of personal turmoil, so he was a bit on edge. Despite all this, he believed he delivered results and deserved to be compensated fairly for his efforts. As he waited for the results, he was keenly aware of the timeline associated with bonus checks being distributed and was becoming increasingly anxious to hear from Rajit.

He started to build a story (in his mind) that Rajit was deliberately withholding the feedback because it was negative, and he wanted to avoid a difficult conversation. Steve repeatedly called HR to find out what was going on. The folks in HR were reluctant to just give him a number, but they finally told him his score and the bonus amount that was linked to it. Needless to say, he wasn't happy. Not only was he disappointed in the amount of money he was going to receive, he was even more upset that he didn't hear it directly from Rajit.

Steve immediately jumped to concluding that Rajit was avoiding sharing the feedback and bonus number, and he was upset that he could neither defend himself nor get answers to his questions. He had been with the company for more than ten years and, in his mind, was a valuable contributor over that period of time. Sure, he didn't have the best year, largely because of his personal circumstances, but he still delivered results. In his words, he felt "stabbed in the back."

To build support for this story, he vented to anyone who would listen, including HR. He wasn't really interested in another perspective; he just wanted people to agree with him.

When Steve told me about the situation during one of our coaching calls, I asked him if he had had the chance to talk directly to his boss yet. He told me he hadn't and didn't think it was worthwhile at this point, since Rajit was so busy transitioning into his new role. I asked him if he was open to the possibility that there may be more going on than what meets the eye. The last one was a hard question for him to consider. Steve had resigned himself to the fact that his story about his boss was the truth, yet he agreed that he needed to call him to find out what was going on. I received a call from Steve about a week later, and here's what he shared with me.

Steve went onto the call with Rajit prepared for battle. The way he described it, he started the call by saying, "Why have you been avoiding me? I found out my bonus amount from HR…nice. The least you could have done was to have told me to my face!" He said what followed was not only humbling but embarrassing.

First, Rajit heard that Steve was hounding HR and venting his situation to many people. Next, Rajit was told not to deliver Steve's performance review directly, because he was in the process of transitioning out of the role and needed to prepare his successor to deliver the feedback. This was very difficult for Rajit, as he really wanted to explain the rationale behind the bonus numbers but needed to do as he was directed. He was told that they would be scheduling a time to sit down with Steve, and at a bare minimum, his notes would be delivered via his successor. Clearly, that did not happen. Rajit was shocked, given their relationship, that Steve would assume the worst. Rajit was especially disturbed by the fact that Steve was spreading this around the company rather than coming directly to him. He admitted to Steve that he should have called him directly, but he was so swamped with the new role, it just kept slipping off his radar screen. They had a very candid discussion, and Steve was left with a greater understanding of all that had occurred.

As Steve and I debriefed the situation, we talked about the impact of his presumptions and anger (that lived like the truth) without seeking other perspectives or facts. Here's what Steve said:

"I wish I would have considered there were other possible perspectives before I jumped down his throat. I also wish I would have had the courage to gather the facts before spending weeks building up a story that was not true. I guess I was feeling so bad about a number of things that had occurred over the past year that my mindset was negative and defeated. I'm still not happy with my bonus, but at least now I understand it, and luckily, I was able to have a good conversation with Rajit and get the truth. And given the fact that he is now the head of the

division, I risked alienating myself from him by jumping to conclusions about his intent. I caused myself more stress than I needed to."

This story demonstrates the negative outcomes of buying into your own story and not leveraging the *Point of View Model*. If Steve would have sought an outside, objective person and asked for another point of view instead of trying to get people to commiserate, he could have avoided the pain and stress of jumping to his own conclusions. Also, he could have done a much better job preparing his mindset to have a high-stakes conversation with his boss.

Here are the steps to leveraging the *Point of View Model*:

1. Find four or five trusted colleagues, peers, family members, or anyone else that can offer you an *objective perspective*. We often refer to these folks as the Board of Directors for your life. (Note: If you don't have such a board of directors, we highly recommend you begin recruiting them now!) Ask them to participate in an independent mindset shifting experiment with you.

2. Share with them the event you encountered. As you tell them about the event, you need to be as clear and factual as possible with your step-by-step description of what occurred. We strongly suggest you describe the event to them in a he said/she said manner. Do not attempt to sway them toward any viewpoint – yours or another. Simply stick with the facts. If you veer from the facts and add your

viewpoint (accidentally or on purpose) into your description of the event, you may taint your colleague's experience of the event and essentially invalidate the whole point of the exercise.

3. Once you've given them an objective recollection of the event, simply ask them what their viewpoint is about the event. You may be surprised by what they say.

Assuming you have discovered varying viewpoints, ask each person what they used as criteria or how they arrived at the story they created. Once you've heard their stories, you now have the tools needed to reconsider your original viewpoint. Keep in mind each of their stories is also not the truth. Can you guess what they might be thinking if they have not read this book? You guessed it – they will likely think that their story is the truth!

Using the Point of View Model

Let's say a peer on your team has a habit of interrupting people, shutting down ideas, and is often moody. (Or at least he occurs that way to you!) From your perspective, he is a jerk and always has been. You are now at the point where you dread working with him, but you are about to collaborate on a highly visible project. You know that you need to find a way to shift your mindset about him, so you decide to try the Point of View Model. While your story (or view) is: "The guy is a jerk," you find out your boss's story is: "He doesn't mean to be abrupt or insensitive. He's very smart and

*really busy, so he comes off as brusque at times."
Another peer in another division of the company has
this perspective: "He is just threatened by you; relax, he
doesn't mean anything by it." Your spouse says: "I've
met him at holiday parties, and he seems to be
uncomfortable with small talk…a bit stiff but definitely
not a jerk."*

So now you've gotten points of view or stories from
your trusted board of directors, and none of them
ended up with a story that matched yours. Hmmm, now
what do you do? How about referring back to the
technique we talked about earlier called *Find Another
Way to Say It* or consider blending several of the methods
we've talked about; it will help!

As you start using the *Point of View Model* regularly, we
are confident you'll start noticing it becomes easier to
put yourself in others' shoes. The easier it gets, the
quicker you'll be able to create more powerful deliberate
mindsets and also prevent yourself from the damage
that might otherwise have occurred had you not learned
about and used this technique.

Create a Game

Have you ever considered playing a game to help shift
your mindset around high-stakes presentations and
conversations? Creating a game to shift your focus away
from diminishing or negative thoughts can be a powerful
approach. Successfully using the "Create a Game"
technique requires being creative and shifting your way of
thinking about situations you are faced with. The game

could involve some pretending. Pick something that you are stuck with or annoyed about. You might find using the *Point of View Model* is a good launching pad to broaden your view of a situation. Considering other perspectives is a good way to start imagining a game! Additionally, finding a mantra or phrase to repeat to yourself is a great way to embed the game into your mindset.

Here are a few examples that illustrate how to create a game:

1. **You are preparing to speak at a conference in front of 500 people.** You don't want to be boring or irrelevant, and your anxiety about the situation is not helping you. What if you created a game called "I'm Going to Win Them Over"? In this game, you pivot away from being self-focused and put your attention on engaging your audience. You shift from being concerned about yourself to being energized about the challenge of winning them over. You know you've won the game when you find yourself engaged with the audience, enjoying the interplay, and completely immersed in the present moment with them.

2. **You have to deliver tough news that includes closing offices and possible relocation for staff.** You have worked with these people for a long time and know the impact this news is going to have on their lives. Even though you are aligned with the decision, you care about the team and are feeling horrible about being the bearer of such bad news. You also know from past experience that when you are overwhelmed with emotion, you tend to shut all

emotions off and come across as callous and uncaring. You are concerned your lack of displaying emotion will hinder your ability to deliver the message, and you might occur as being less than empathetic – not the way you want to be perceived. What if you created a game called "Change Can Create Possibilities for People"? In this game, you go into conversations with a deep awareness and confidence that each person will be able to embrace this change, and there may be a wealth of opportunity for them on the other side. While this game will not guarantee the outcome, it will free your mind to be fully present, and in turn help you demonstrate empathy while delivering the tough message. You know you've won the game when you remain grounded, empathetic, and confident in delivering this tough news.

Jeff's Game – The Gratitude Factor

How do you feel when sending a check to Uncle Sam? Angry, bitter, resigned? How about grateful? Unlike the other stories focusing on clients I've coached, this one is about me and a powerful mindset shift that returned me to a feeling of gratitude. This story also demonstrates the power of being able to shift your mindset in the broader context of your life. While I wasn't preparing for a high-stakes conversation, the positive outcome of this story benefits me to this very day. This deliberate shift in mindset happened shortly after I established The Speaker's Choice.

> *My second year in business started out strong; new work was coming in at a rate I never expected. By the end of*

the first quarter, we had booked nearly as much revenue as we did the entire year prior. You'd think I'd be overjoyed by this, but April 15th was not far off, and a nagging voice in my head kept saying, "The more money we make, the more we are going to have to pay Uncle Sam!" That negative internal dialogue was not helping me feel anything remotely close to gratitude. Revisiting the question posed at the beginning of this section: "How do you feel when writing out a check to Uncle Sam? Angry, bitter, resigned?" I was definitely experiencing a bit of all of those three feelings, and it was certainly negatively impacting my mindset.

Something had to change. I thought about the reasons why I was in this particular business, and what my end game was. Without hesitation, I reminded myself of our amazing team, the great clients we got to work with, our flourishing business, and having more than enough opportunities for all of us to thrive. As I reflected on the course of my career from being an engineer who had become bored to now owning a business and being in charge of my own destiny, it hit me! In that moment, I felt an immense amount of gratitude for everything in my life…well…almost everything. Guess who came to mind again? Uncle Sam. "How am I going to deal with my negative mindset around that?"

Then the idea of "Find Another Way to Say It" popped into my head. So I started with: "Like it or not, Uncle Sam IS entitled to his fair share." Then, I decided to look up personal income tax rates in a few other countries around the world. Some of the Scandinavian countries pay nearly 20% more than we do in the United States!

That difference occurred to me as enormous, so much so, that it stopped me in my tracks and shaped my next version of Find Another Way to Say It, which was: "WOW… I am so grateful to be paying 20% less in taxes than I would be paying if I lived in some other countries." Believe it or not, that did it for me. I was able to quickly shift my mindset from bitterness to gratitude. But the game didn't end there.

I also decided that I would make a game out of putting money aside for taxes at the end of the year. I created a game that involved the account that was earmarked for paying taxes. I deposited a larger amount than had been recommended by our CPA, but then pretended that the smaller, recommended sum, had been deposited. We set it up like an automatic deposit. I didn't pay attention to it, and had almost forgotten the account was set up. The positive, unexpected impact at tax time was that we had a lot more money in the account than we needed to pay our taxes. It may seem silly, but it was effective for me! My ability to turn this game into positive momentum around the growth of our company has had a long-standing ripple effect.

FINAL THOUGHTS ON CREATING A DELIBERATE MINDSET

The key word in this step is *deliberate*. It's not always easy to consciously choose a different mindset; it takes resolve and a belief that the shift to a more powerful perspective will make a difference. We have witnessed our clients create deliberate mindsets countless times and have been blown away by the powerful results they experienced as a result of their efforts – we know it works. The next chapter highlights some of our favorites! It is our hope that the ideas, tools, and stories shared here will spark ideas within you to deal with your **own** default mindsets. We know this is just the tip of the iceberg when it comes to finding ways to shift. Our encouragement to you is to do *something*. Start small and practice when it doesn't count!

CHAPTER 6

MINDSET IN ACTION: STORIES OF OVERCOMING NEGATIVE DEFAULT MINDSETS

The following stories highlight specific coaching situations in which we have been able to help our clients overcome negative default mindsets. Through their hard work and dedication to the process, they were able to achieve new levels of confidence and effectiveness in their personal high-stakes situations. Our goal is to give you a glimpse into our coaching process and inspire you with the stories of real people being able to put the process of shifting mindset into action. As you read, you'll notice we sometimes employ multiple techniques to achieve the desired outcome. While there are many other important components that need to be mastered to generate a high level of presence, you will see that very often what *truly* hinders each of these professionals is an underlying mindset that needs to change.

We offer our clients a variety of training and coaching options that include group and one-on-one sessions. As such, we offer accounts from our respective experiences. We begin with Jeff's coaching narratives and then move on to Sue's. We hope these stories resonate with you and offer insights or ideas on how to address any negative mindsets that might be holding you back!

Coaching Stories from Jeff

The Terrified Speaker Gives a Speech

Kristine is a highly skilled consultant specializing in the foodservice industry. Her track record of success afforded her access to high-level leadership in several major companies. Those companies relied on Kristine and her team to open doors for them to one of the world's largest fast food chains. Since she and her team were a key connection point, the relationships Kristine developed were extremely valuable. She was comfortable having boardroom meetings with clients in their offices – hashing through issues, presenting data, and discussing strategy.

As an upcoming annual foodservice conference was being planned (an event that draws up to 1500 people), a group of client companies reached out to Kristine and invited her to be the keynote speaker. The idea terrified her.

Kristine had never delivered a formal speech to any group. Her meetings were always centered on showing results of different processes, recommending new strategies, and answering questions. These situations were within the realm of her expertise and conversational in tone, not a formal presentation to 1500 people. So she told them, "Thanks, but no thanks!"

When Kristine passed on the invitation, her clients asked her to reconsider. They pushed hard on the idea that the people attending the keynote were eager to hear her insightful thought leadership. They reminded her if she presented, the buzz would certainly draw interest and likely an influx of consulting opportunities for her firm. Sheepishly, she finally agreed and called me to help.

During our first session, I asked Kristine how she wanted to be perceived by this 1500-person audience. She used words like: confident, knowledgeable, passionate, and engaging. She quickly followed up these descriptors by expressing her fear which was making it very difficult to believe that she could EVER live up to those expectations. Often clients enter this process with a mindset of "I'm really bad at this kind of thing," or, as Kristine put it, "I'm terrified about speaking to a large group." In fact, she admitted that it took her several weeks to get up the nerve to call me! I acknowledged her worries and courage for finally picking up the phone, then let her know she was not alone.

We got to work with our usual process, including lots of video recording, feedback, course correction, and repetition. As expected, she exhibited a lot of nervousness: a shaking voice, very minimal pausing, saying too many filler words (um, uh, ya know), and fidgeting with her hands the whole time. During this phase of coaching, we also reinforce an individual's strengths, as this is pivotal in creating a solid foundation for an empowering mindset. Kristine was able to see what I saw: she had reasonably solid posture and good eye contact. This was the launching pad for a shift in mindset for her, because she got to see that she wasn't as bad as she thought she was!

For many of our clients, seeing themselves on video for the first time in a professional setting can be unnerving, revealing, and, in some cases, pleasantly surprising. Reactions vary. Following are some of Kristine's comments after a handful of video recordings and playbacks. These comments are very typical and representative of many client reactions: "I can't believe it; I really didn't look anywhere near as nervous as I felt." "Wow, I was certain I'd hear my voice cracking a lot, but that wasn't the case at all." By taking Kristine through the process of seeing a different perspective outside her own and trusting the process, we paved the way for her to consider shifting her mindset away from her disempowering view of herself.

To reinforce Kristine's initial perceptions of her first video playback, I began giving her feedback on the strengths I saw and how they tied into her desired perceptions. Her combined strengths of balanced posture and her eye contact helped her to convey confidence and appear engaging. Remember earlier in the book that we talked about two techniques called *Envision a Future State* and *Find Another Way to Say It*? I introduced these techniques to Kristine, and we started working on them right away. Here are a few that Kristine created:

- "I am more prepared than I've ever been in my life…for anything!"

- "I'm a human being; they're human beings, so it's all going to be okay."

- "My audience wants me to succeed as much as I do!"

Over the course of a few months, Kristine shifted her mindset dramatically and was able to start envisioning how her future presentation would go. During one of our last sessions, I asked Kristine to reflect back to the time when she was too nervous to even call me, and compare that to her current mindset about presenting on a stage to 1500 people. She said, "I know I can do it, and this is such a huge professional step for me." To help her reinforce how far she had come in her development in this area, I asked her to list some of the top insights from our coaching and to keep the list handy in case she needed a reminder. Following are her top four comments:

1. I would have never guessed this, but I really have shifted my mindset away from "silence is awkward," to "I embrace silence, and it's a good thing!" It is such a powerful tool that has helped me stay composed, especially in the face of high-stakes presentations, and has helped my audiences to stay engaged.

2. I am getting to a level of unconscious competence with the skills, and I do not really have to think about them too often. I'm delivering better presentations and having better interactions with my clients already.

3. I feel more confident than ever before about how to structure my content, target my presentations to the audience, and deliver my message in a logical, clear, concise manner.

4. One of my peers told me I was among the top-rated speakers at a recent conference. In a million years, I'd never have expected to hear that.

In the days leading up to the keynote, Kristine created a couple of additional mantras that she repeated every time she started feeling that twinge of nervousness. These mantras helped Kristine create the grounded, confident, and clear mindset she was seeking. And as you might expect, she did a phenomenal job!

From Sweaty Palms to Director

The first time I met Dan, he said, "Look at my hands right now…we haven't even started the coaching, and just the thought of working with you is getting my palms all sweaty." This was my introduction to Dan – an extremely bright, technical expert who worked for a Fortune 500 company in a very competitive environment and who was on the cusp of either being promoted or getting fired! In fact, he failed his first round of "Director Candidate" presentations, because his presentation skills were so abysmal. One of the comments made by the executive leadership team (ELT) was that Dan's excessive sweating was beyond distracting. Luckily, the ELT believed in Dan, so they decided to give him one more chance. They implored him to get a coach to improve his executive presence before meeting with them again.

During our first session, I asked Dan to further describe the challenging situation he was facing. He talked about his firm's grueling promotion process and that the ELT had a very high bar for executive presence. He would need to deliver a short, 15-minute presentation describing his value proposition, followed by five minutes of Q & A. When I asked him how he was feeling about working together, he responded, "I'm REALLY hoping you can work your magic on me and can help me pass this next round. As you'll soon see, I am really horrible at presenting. If you can't tell, this is MAJOR high stakes for me. If I fail again, I'll likely be let go. To add to the pressure I'm feeling, my wife is freaking out about this too; we have two kids and a house in the burbs, so she's feeling insecure at the moment."

Wow! He revealed a lot and painted a great picture of where his mindset was. I let him know that he was in good hands, and if he was willing to push himself beyond his comfort zone, he would see results.

Knowing that our work would entail lots of video recording and coaching on the **mechanics,** along with some coaching on his **messaging,** I wanted to start chipping away at his negative default mindset.

Since he was used to direct feedback, I said, "Dan, I get that you think you are a poor presenter, so we're going to start video-recording and playing the clips back so we can start to identify what is and isn't working for you. Before we start, I'm going to strongly suggest from this moment forward, you stop going down the negative mindset path. I want to help you create a more positive and deliberate mindset with a technique we call: *Find Another Way to Say It.* Got it?" I told him that very often the conversations we have in our heads predetermine what the outcomes will be, and from what I could tell so far, his conversations were not empowering. I let him know that I would coach him through different ways to improve the conversations he was having with himself as we began the video recording process.

When we took a coffee break, he said, "I really do appreciate the ELT giving me a second chance, and as much as I don't like presenting, I'm glad to be getting this coaching." This was a start – he was already putting a positive spin on things!

I don't recall the exact number, but we probably recorded Dan at least 15 times during our first session. He delivered mini-presentations on various topics, so I could give him specific skill-building exercises designed to address the feedback from the ELT. As we played back the recordings, I asked Dan to comment each time, but he wasn't allowed to say: "I am horrible at presenting." He needed to be honest with himself, trust my feedback, and start *Finding Another Way to Say It* when he truly saw some improvement. Dan progressed from:

> *"I am horrible at presenting"* to:
> *"I feel very uncomfortable"* to:
> *"While I don't think I'm good at presenting, I think the coaching will help me improve."*

He eventually got to:

> "The ELT gave me another chance; I'm going to take full advantage of the opportunity I've been given to work with my coach. My goal is to surprise the ELT with my improved executive presence and get promoted to Director."

You get the point. I reminded him again of the need to set ourselves up for success and how the conversations in our heads predetermine what the outcomes will be.

Over the next few months, I noticed Dan had increasingly improved his ability to shift his mindset when he noticed it was going south. He began to stop himself when a negative thought would arise and shift to a more positive thought which, from my perspective as his coach, was awesome to see!

One other obstacle he needed to overcome was "sounding too scripted." He needed to shift from presenting formally to being more conversational. To help him do this, I asked him to share some of his favorite memories of his childhood. When he did this, he looked and sounded much more relaxed. I asked him how he could take this conversational tone into his "Director Candidate" presentation. He said, "Well, I think I should keep working on those *Find Another Way to Say It* things you told me to do and create one that helps me be more conversational, like: I'm more prepared than ever to talk with the ELT in a conversational way. They believe in me enough to give me another chance, so I intend to put my focus on them and not worry so much about myself." He got it!

Our coaching sessions went on for nearly four months. It took a long time, but Dan finally got to a point where he really believed he'd have a legitimate shot at getting promoted.

On the day of his presentation, he felt confident. When he called me, it was clear that he had nailed it. He said the ELT asked him what he had done to improve, because this presentation was significantly better than last time; he didn't really look like the same person. He told them he had taken their advice and hired a coach. Dan experienced the power of video feedback and creating a positive, deliberate mindset by succeeding in a high-stakes presentation. He was ultimately promoted to director. Furthermore, he continued to leverage these skills with his team and his ongoing personal and professional growth.

Mother Knows Best

A long-time client and executive leader reached out to talk about an individual on his team he felt needed coaching. Carter didn't know exactly what Melissa needed, but he framed it under the heading of "communication skills" coaching.

According to Carter, Melissa was technically competent in her role as SVP of Finance. Furthermore, she always received praise from other leaders in the organization as well as from her peers for doing a great job – not only for the quality of her work but also for being on time (usually early) and under budget. He also indicated that she was open to feedback.

Despite these strengths, Melissa needed to put more focus on relating to people and building relationships. He received feedback that she had difficulty making connections with her peers, and he observed she was even more challenged when she presented upward within the organization or externally to clients or potential clients. Additionally, her style often occurred as too formal, sometimes condescending, and judgmental.

The Coaching Begins:

I began by asking about her perspective on making connections with people at work. Her response was, "My focus at work has always been on the numbers and strategy. In my opinion, that's where it should be, don't you think? I was hired to create and execute our financial strategy, not to make friends at work. Obviously, if this was the first thing Carter told you, it must be important to him. I wonder if more than a few other people have noticed this but didn't say anything."

I told her that this would be an area for us to explore further as the coaching progressed. I was both surprised and encouraged by how direct she was – this demonstrated that she had no issue expressing her point of view!

I wanted to know more about how she reacted when co-workers wanted to make small talk or learn more about her. What she said was revealing and helped me begin to understand her default mindset:

"I don't like it, especially when people are trying to dig into my personal life. I'm a private person, and as I said before, I'm here to work, not make friends. One thing I've noticed at work that bothers me is that people talk too much. I don't have time to listen to all that chatter. It seems like a lot of worthless conversations happen – not just around here, but also at the other firms I've worked for in the past. I'm certain if people would spend less time talking and more time doing, more would get accomplished in a lot less time. Work time is supposed to be for working, not socializing. I know this probably sounds harsh, but people know me at this point, so they

*don't bother trying to engage with me about anything
other than business – which I think is best."*

I sat back and thought about what she said. While I
understood where she was coming from, her comments
triggered something. For the first time, I could easily see
how others perceived her as judgmental, arrogant, and
aloof. Who would want to connect with someone like
that? Additionally, if she was a private person and didn't
share much about her personal life, how could anyone
get to know her?

I wanted to help Melissa reveal a potential blind spot.
Therefore, Melissa's first homework assignment was to
make notes on whatever came to her mind when she
considered what she may be missing out on by keeping
the barriers between her and her colleagues. Being
analytically minded, she wanted to know how this would
make an impact, and she was initially skeptical about the
approach. I encouraged her to trust in the process, and
she agreed to do the homework. It wasn't long before I
received an email from her asking if we could move our
next session to an earlier date, because she wanted to
share some things she had discovered while doing her
homework. I rearranged a few things and told her I
couldn't wait to hear what she had to say.

When we met for our coaching session, I could sense
something different about her way of being and
suspected that she had discovered something powerful.
She revealed that she had struggled trying to determine
what she might be missing out on by putting up barriers
with her colleagues. Nothing came to mind until she
reached out to her mother, a former corporate executive

and informal mentor to Melissa throughout her career. She trusted her mother's judgment and opinion, so she sent her an email describing our coaching engagement and her first homework assignment. Her mother sent back the following email, which Melissa shared with me.

Melissa -

I'm so glad you reached out and shared that you are working with a coach. I am very pleased for you, as I think this is a pivotal point in your career. Last time we spoke, you told me that you are always exhausted and never have time or energy for anything outside of work. You also shared that you think no one can do your job as well as you can, and therefore, you haven't been willing to give up control or start trying to delegate. With that approach, you're not only stifling your subordinates' growth, but you're also getting in the way of building trust with them. If you don't develop your team and create some bench strength, you won't be doing the right thing for the organization in the long run.

One thing I can tell you, based upon my 30+ years of leadership experience, is that relationships DO matter. There are a million examples of how the personal relationships and trust I developed with people over the course of my career allowed me to navigate or avoid a myriad of issues that came up on a day-to-day basis. Take time to work on this – it will not only pay off for your career, but it will make your work more enjoyable and filled with purpose.

After I finished reading, I looked up at Melissa who appeared to be speechless. She finally spoke up and said, "I'm blown away. I can't believe I was blind to all of this. I think my mother has been trying to tell me this for years; how did I miss it?"

We talked about the fact that, over time, she had developed a really strong default mindset that her way was the right way, and unless she was willing to consider what her mother told her, nothing could or would change. Thankfully, she was willing and made the choice to shift to a more deliberate mindset. I knew how hard this was for her and told her how proud I was of her openness and commitment to growth. She could now get to work and begin the process of creating a new deliberate mindset.

Her next assignment was to capture any thoughts or insights about what she could start doing differently. She took it seriously, and over the course of several sessions, we developed a list of specific actions she could begin to employ:

1. Get time on Carter's calendar soon to share her insights and ask if he'd be willing to be an accountability partner to support her development of some new skills.

2. During the course of meetings when non-work-related items come up, stick her toe in the water and participate in the conversation.

3. Begin to reveal what she has discovered from the coaching homework with people at work. Be willing to be vulnerable!

4. Create a few mantras to help shift her mindset when she is feeling unsure about how to approach a situation. For example: Be open and willing to share; being curious about others is a good thing; it's ok to show vulnerability and humanity!

5. Use the *Stop-Challenge-Choose* method when she notices she is about to say something she might regret later. BREATHE!

It probably isn't a surprise that Melissa applied her diligent work ethic to our coaching, and, as a result, she experienced a phenomenal shift in her life – both inside and outside of work. In follow-up conversations with Carter, he shared that over the course of a year, he had seen many positive changes in Melissa. Equally as important, her team and senior leadership responded to her differently, and she continued to progress as a leader. The impetus for her growth was her willingness to seek out and listen to other perspectives. And if all else fails, when you're stuck and don't know what to do, pick up the phone and call your *mom!*

The Skeptic Changes His Ways

Remember when we mentioned getting a board of directors for your life? This is a story about one of *my* board members, Ken. Ken and I meet regularly to support and coach one another in various personal and business pursuits. During one of our regular Saturday morning breakfasts, Ken mentioned the idea of refinancing his existing home mortgage to reduce the interest rate, which we both agreed was way too high. I encouraged Ken to call a mutual colleague in the mortgage business. Being a skeptic and a little reactionary, he immediately hemmed and hawed at the idea. He ultimately took my advice, called the broker, and was excited to learn he'd likely be able to drop his current interest rate as much as 2%. He called me two days later to share the good news.

The good news only lasted a short time as he began to recall a prior refinancing experience which led him to complaining about how much time and energy it took to gather up all the paperwork – from tax returns, pay stubs, other existing debt, credit verification, childcare expenses, etc. Just the thought of all that work amped him up, "I can't go through this ordeal again. The broker told me it was *likely* I'd be able to get the rate drop. That's no guarantee! Maybe I'll just forget about the refi." Given our relationship, I called him out on the negative default mindset he was creating around the refi process. I told him to chill a bit and go calculate how much money he could save if he could cut his interest rate as much as 2% – maybe that would inspire him to continue! I asked if he was open to some coaching and to hearing my thoughts about his reaction. He took a deep breath and reluctantly agreed.

I began by pointing out how quickly he convinced himself that this refinance deal would be as painful as the one in the past. This was a perfect time to talk with him about the assumptions he was making and share the *Stop-Challenge-Choose* model. I wanted him to STOP his ranting and CHALLENGE the assumptions he was making about how difficult the refi process would be. I suggested he stop making assumptions about how this would turn out and encouraged him to start challenging his auto-response and CHOOSE a different way of thinking before he decided to move ahead or stop the loan process. He needed to take time to think about this and envision how he would feel about the benefits of completing the loan process, the least of which was being able to dedicate extra money toward other important things. I encouraged him to invoke the *24-Hour Rule* before he decided what to do.

We reconnected a few days later, and he shared his thoughts. He admitted that he understood he was collapsing his past and current experiences and realized his assumptions were just that – assumptions, not facts. He recognized that it would be smarter not to assume this experience would be like it was last time. I agreed and suggested the mortgage industry was very different than it was several years ago. The people were different, the process was likely a little different, and technology would be different.

I suggested that if he wanted to assume things, how about creating a deliberate mindset that assumed something different and positive? What about creating an expectation that he would have a **good** experience? I shared with him that I used to have similar thoughts about expecting things to be difficult or challenging, and the result was often a self-fulfilling prophecy. Once I discovered the power of creating a deliberate mindset, I noticed things seemed to turn out in my favor more than ever before. I challenged him to test my advice and see what he noticed. He appreciated my insights and told me he would give it a try.

As Ken moved forward in the process, scanning and emailing what seemed like 5,000 documents, the laborious underwriting process began. Receiving weekly updates from his mortgage broker, everything seemed to be progressing smoothly. Then the first estimated closing date came and went. Getting a little concerned, Ken reached out to his broker for assurance. Following several exchanges, Ken's broker left this message: "I'm very concerned we have not heard from the bank. If I were you, I would call the county recorder's office and see if they can help you."

He instantly slipped back into his default mindset of "Oh no, here we go again!" Followed by, "Are you kidding me? I just *knew* I'd have to deal with those morons at some point. They don't care; they're just collecting a paycheck. I'll be dealing with these idiots for days, and we'll get nothing accomplished!"

As Ken picked up the phone and began to dial, he recognized his slip back into the negative default mindset. He had an expectation of the person on the other end of the phone – he/she would be a lifetime government employee, rude, dismissive, and someone who thought of taxpayers as troublemakers. Ken conjured up that image in a split second while dialing. Can you relate?

At that moment, BANG! Something shifted for Ken. He stopped dialing and considered how much his negative mindset could have been impeding his ability to have things go his way more often. He knew his old way of thinking had no power. He changed his internal dialogue to something like this:

"I will have a positive experience with the person from the recorder's office who takes my call, and this person will help me resolve my issue quickly and to my full satisfaction."

Not surprising to me, it worked! A very professional woman answered the phone. She was courteous, competent, and super helpful. Ken was beyond satisfied. He made a point to tell her that his experience with her was a bright spot in his day. Later that day, he received an email that indicated everything was now in order – he was on his way to closing on a new mortgage.

There is great power in being able to take the reins on negative thought patterns. Ken's ability to cool off enabled him to approach a simple conversation differently – and the outcome was positive. The key is to recognize what your triggers are and to be willing to interrupt the process.

Coaching Stories from Sue

Derailed by a Default Mindset

Mark had been recently hired at a high-profile, investment-banking firm. He had an MBA with seven years of experience in the industry. In his new, client-facing role, Mark wanted to get more comfortable speaking with clients and thinking quickly on his feet. He was an expert in his field, but he struggled to effectively articulate his firm's value proposition. Not only was he struggling, he was basically mute in high-stakes client meetings, and this was not going to help him progress to partner status.

As we worked together in the first few sessions, Mark thought his biggest challenges were his difficulties with: crafting a good message, standing up straight, looking people in the eye, and learning to stop saying *um*. He was stunned when he discovered the biggest hindrance to his success did not reside in those issues. His biggest difficulty was the underlying default mindset that was setting him up for failure every time he found himself in high-stakes conversations with his superiors and clients. Here's how we uncovered it.

During one of our first sessions, I asked why he was holding back during client meetings. He said things like, "I guess I feel like I need to know everything about a subject to contribute, and if I don't feel like I have anything to contribute, I just say nothing…and I know that's not going to cut it for long."

I wondered how he could doubt his knowledge, given his MBA and previous seven years of experience, and asked him why he felt like he didn't have enough knowledge to contribute.

He responded, "It's not that I don't know anything; it's that I don't know everything. I really want to know an industry inside and out before I assert myself as an expert. I just want to make sure I'm asking smart questions, and I don't think I have any real value to add above and beyond what the senior guys in the room are already saying. But I know that by being mute, I'm not doing myself any favors either."

When I asked if he thought the others in the room had more knowledge than he did, he replied, "Not necessarily, they are just more comfortable thinking quickly on their feet. They have a lot more confidence and presence than I do."

Even though Mark had great experience, an MBA from a leading institution, and beat out 25 others for his job, he still didn't think he had the right to be sitting at the table. I asked him if he had always been so hard on himself.

Mark told me that when he was in high school, he was on the debate team and got good grades. His mom pushed him hard. If he came home with an A, she asked why he didn't get an A+. He grew up thinking that no matter how well he did, he could always know more and do better. While this belief fueled his drive and performance in many areas of his life, it also had a downside.

Just like that, Mark had identified his default mindset: Even though there was evidence pointing to the fact that he was smart and competent, in his mind, he didn't believe he deserved to be there.

Clearly, this default mindset was not serving Mark. Now that he had recognized it, he needed to replace that belief with a more empowering deliberate mindset.

How many of you can see yourself in Mark? Despite evidence to the contrary, Mark had a belief about himself that wasn't serving him. I suggested that he use the *Point of View Model* to seek out other perspectives – a personal 360-degree feedback mission. He decided it would be helpful to talk to people inside his organization as well as others with whom he had worked in the past and former classmates from his MBA program. He structured his questions to get at their perception of his engagement at the onset of projects as well as when he was a new member of a team. As he received the feedback, a common theme emerged. Here's a summary of what Mark learned:

> *Mark is a great listener and thinker. You can often see the wheels turning and can tell he is coming up with a different perspective that could be just what the group needs. However, he rarely shares his thoughts during group meetings. He waits for casual settings after meetings to reveal his analysis or point of view. Almost every perspective he shares is brilliant…he needs to speak up more when it counts!*

When Mark revealed that he heard a slightly different version of this statement several times, he realized that his default mindset of "having to know everything" or "be the expert to earn the right to contribute" was not serving him, and it wasn't serving the group either.

Over time, he gained more confidence putting forth his ideas and point of view in client meetings. This mindset shift, combined with fine-tuning his delivery skills, made a huge difference for Mark and his career.

He Changed His Reputation

Having self-awareness (however you get it) is vital to one's personal and professional development. In fact, people are often so unaware that they usually don't see a need for improvement, even after a boss has provided them with a coach to help them develop!

Peter, the founder of a small consulting firm we've worked with over the years, wanted me to coach a new employee they had recently hired, James. Based on his extensive client-facing experience, James was brought into the organization as a billable consultant. He came in selling himself as a big rainmaker. Unfortunately, James wasn't making it rain.

Peter thought James was too full of himself, a whiner, and a complainer. Peter asked me to diagnose the situation and determine how best to work with him.

During our first session, James told me he felt like his head was on the chopping block. He indicated that he had several high-stakes conversations with the founder of the firm, and none of them went well. Then he went into all the reasons why.

His perception was that the firm wasn't supporting him as much as they could be. He was in a remote location, and as a result, he thought no one at the firm cared about him, so he felt neglected. No one was coaching him. He wasn't being brought before high-profile clients, and he felt like he was on his own.

Although some of his complaints were based on facts, it was obvious that James was ruled by negativity, and I was suspicious of a default mindset lurking in there somewhere. During the next several sessions, we went about discovering what it was.

Because an individual's self-perception is just one data point, it is crucial they hear how other people perceive them as well. Like most coaches, we regularly use self-assessments and a 360-type of interview process to determine how our clients are perceived by others within their organizations. After reviewing James' self-assessments and 360 feedback, we assembled these data points:

1.   James was competitive, which would most often be considered a strength in a sales-oriented role. However, when overplayed, this strength led to problems when he tried to build relationships.

2.   James also had a very strong moral compass and expected others to have similar morals and values. There was a perception that James had only one way to see things, and if others didn't agree with his opinion, James felt he wasn't being supported.

3.   There was a recurrent theme in the 360-interviews that he complained a lot and was constantly finding problems.

His strengths served him well from the standpoint of integrity with clients. Unfortunately, when it came to dealing with his associates, James would complain to whoever would listen and commiserate with him about the way things were done. He was beginning to build a negative reputation.

I gave James this feedback on our third call; this is where the breakthrough happened. James clearly saw that he was creating the reputation of being a victim. He tied it back to his early years growing up. He recalled many situations in which he felt he witnessed injustices and wrongdoing in the way his stepfather treated their family. He wasn't supported financially to go to college, and when he left home, he had to completely fend for himself.

Although he realized this grit had made him successful in the past, it occurred to him that it might now be getting in the way of his integration into this new culture. Once he had this realization, he could consider letting go of the fight, and he could see the possibility of another way to get what he needed. At this point, he declared his intent to shift his negative default mindset into one that was more empowering and sustainable.

We set out to help James create a new and deliberate mindset. We used the *Point of View Model* for a couple of James' hot-button issues in which he felt unsupported. Based on the feedback I heard, I coached James to consider other perspectives of his situation.

James clearly saw that he was judging people based on his own perception. He was getting in their faces and digging in his heels. These types of behaviors were contributing to his bad reputation.

Luckily, an upcoming, company-wide meeting at the corporate office would give him the perfect opportunity to put his new deliberate mindset into practice and begin the process of changing his reputation within the company. This would be James' first face-to-face meeting with many of his co-workers, and it would be an opportunity for him to show up as a different person. It felt high-stakes for James; he knew this was going to be his one shot to change how people perceived him.

To help him think about how he wanted to be perceived, I asked him to list all the great attributes he brings to an organization and the people he works with. He listed some awesome qualities: passion, love for his clients, generosity with all members of his team – all of these were commendable attributes.

Was he perceived that way? No. We needed to get his mindset to a place where he could authentically show up as himself – without trying too hard to prove himself.

He knew that he wasn't going to be able to show up and proclaim, "Hey, guys, I'm passionate, I'm service oriented, and I am here to help any way I can!" He had to demonstrate it.

We talked about strategies to help him shift his mindset to a confident and empowered place, so he could demonstrate these qualities naturally, not in a forced way. To do this, James spent time envisioning who he needed to be, how he would behave, and how he wanted to be perceived at the meeting.

One of the other techniques he used during the week leading up to the meeting was to repeat the following mantras to himself: "I'm not going to talk about myself. I'm going to ask a lot of questions. I'm not the smartest guy in the room. I'm there for others. I'm there to get to know other people and be of service to them."

The morning of the meeting, he set aside an extra fifteen minutes before leaving his hotel room to meditate and breathe. He did this to calm any last-minute nerves before entering the ballroom to meet many of his colleagues in person for the first time.

I received a text from the founder of the firm within five minutes of the meeting's close, which read: "Who was this guy that showed up today? Outstanding! He was awesome, and everyone loved him. It was great."

Thirty minutes later came a text from James: "It was just fabulous. I was very skeptical of the process you asked me to go through, because at first it didn't seem tangible. Whatever it was – it worked, because I felt relaxed. I was having fun, and people really did get to see the side of me that I so wanted them to see."

People often get in their own way without even knowing it. If you can open up to the possibility that there are always others ways to view a situation, you'll be amazed to discover a whole new world of options and approaches. From there, great strides can be made to shift your mindset and deliver more powerfully and effectively than before.

The Dreaded Feedback Conversation

Feedback conversations can feel very high-stakes to both managers and employees. Often dreaded by both, yet absolutely necessary, these conversations provide a prime opportunity for many to succeed or fail.

After a workshop for one of our clients, Natalie, a senior manager, called me. She needed to give sensitive feedback to one of the younger members of her team. Zach was not only new to the team, he was also young, and this was his first "real job" in a professional environment.

Natalie described Zach as bright and very eager, but he came across as a know-it-all, interrupted a lot, and others on the team were starting to get upset. They were giving her negative feedback about him, and she knew she had to follow up. She called me for some advice on how to handle this conversation. She had tried to give him feedback in the past, and it hadn't gone well. Not only did the actual conversation not go well, she never saw any behavioral change. She was uncomfortable and nervous at the thought of another conversation going the same way. She knew she needed to do something different this time, so she asked for some coaching.

During our initial conversation, it became clear this situation was going to address more than how to structure a feedback conversation. In one of the workshops we had conducted with Natalie's team, we had talked about effective ways to give feedback and provided cues that can be used to help the person receiving the feedback to be a little more receptive. She seemed to have a good handle on that, so I started to think that the underlying issues might be mindset related.

I asked how she felt about delivering feedback to people on her team. She indicated that she rarely gave feedback unless there was a problem, and because the nature of these conversations was often strife with bad news, they caused her anxiety.

When I asked her why she struggled to give negative feedback, she said she didn't like to be perceived as the heavy. She wanted to be liked and to feel like she was a good manager. She wanted to motivate her team and was concerned that negative feedback would be interpreted as a lack of faith in them.

We switched gears at that point. I asked her to think about Zach and whether or not she believed in him.

That question opened a new line of thinking for Natalie, and she started talking about all the positive things about him and the potential she saw. If he could overcome these negative traits, he could possibly be fast-tracked to a promotion, and begin attending client meetings.

I asked her to think about one of the things we talked about in the workshop: When employees receive negative feedback, they often become triggered. I asked what she thought some of Zach's triggers might be.

She said that she thought his confidence and eagerness might lead him to be defensive, and ultimately, he might then question the validity of her feedback. This line of thinking led her right back into the mindset of being nervous about having the feedback conversation, because she didn't know how to deal with the possibility of him questioning her.

The first thing we did was review the *Point of View Model*. We tweaked the model a bit to help expand Natalie's perspective on Zach. Rather than put HER point of view in the center, we placed the point of view other people had about Zach in the center: He was a know-it-all, stepped on people's toes, and was irritating to his colleagues.

I then asked her to think about other perspectives of Zach and to begin populating the different aspects of the model that represent different points of view from the one in the center – the most negative point of view. As she started to think about this, she actually began describing him through the lens of strength. He was always the most prompt, the most reliable, and the most prepared for meetings. He might occur as a little bit impatient, since it appeared other people didn't seem to be as prepared as he was. He might not currently be a good listener, but that didn't mean that he isn't capable of being one. She went through this model and started to see there were many different perspectives of him apart from the ones she had heard from the team.

We paused for her to digest everything we had discussed, the information she wanted to tell him, and the feedback from other people on the team. After going through the *Point of View Model*, she felt a lot more at ease, because she wasn't hyper-focused on the negative. She now had a full picture of him. Therefore, she felt more confident in her ability to speak with him. She was no longer concerned about being perceived as the bad guy, because she had his best interest in mind.

That was the breakthrough moment for Natalie. She said, "You know what? Someone has to tell him this. I'm the closest one to him, and I know the most; it has to be me. I don't care if he likes me or not; I'm doing this for him, because I care about him and his career."

Then we talked about preparing for the conversation that would take place a few days later. She captured all the descriptors of her point of view she had about him, and we talked about actual language that she could use in her upcoming conversation with Zach.

For this, we used the *Find Another Way to Say It* technique. How could she say it better so that he might hear it better? How could she say, "You're aggravating and annoying people; you're perceived as a know-it-all."? She knew that in order for him to build trust with people on the team, he needed to stop trying so hard to prove himself, and begin focusing on earning the right to be heard. To do that, he had to take the focus off himself and have a lower self-orientation. She used this logic to find a better way to deliver the message. Here's what she came up with:

> *"I want you to begin to focus on building trust with people on the team beyond your technical competence. It is clear to me (and everyone else) that you are smart. What isn't clear is whether or not you are willing to listen and learn from others. That's where I need you to put your focus."*

Next, Natalie needed to prepare her mindset for the conversation. She wanted to create a mantra or two to remind herself of the following things: She knows and feels she is a confident manager; feedback is a gift, and it is essential Zach hears this feedback. Together we came up with positive mantras to help her. She wrote them down and placed them in front of her to help boost her confidence.

Before the conversation, Natalie incorporated meditation time. She made sure she took fifteen minutes with her door shut to just sit quietly, breathe, and repeat some of those mantras, so she would be mentally prepared for the conversation. She had all her facts written out. She knew what she needed to say. This was the time to clear her mind and remind herself of why she was doing it.

Then she was ready. She had the tools and the mindset to clearly communicate. She told Zach that he could be a role model for other people on the team, but there were some aspects of his behavior that were holding him back and causing him to lose credibility. She gave him permission to focus on building relationships with the team, so he could earn their trust and confidence. Doing so would not only bolster his credibility on the team, it would also win him more interface time with clients. She offered to coach him if he needed to gain awareness of what he was doing, what he needed to stop doing, and what he needed to start doing to improve.

She told him if he could do these things, he would be unstoppable. That really got his attention! She told me that this was a turning point in the conversation, because he finally took responsibility. He told her the following:

"I know what you're talking about, and I can feel it when I'm doing it. I feel this burning urge to jump in, because I get irritated when someone misses a key point or gets something wrong." Bingo. He just became conscious of his incompetence!

At this point, they were able to get beyond his defensiveness and get to the heart of the matter. What else could he do when that feeling came up for him? Natalie easily transitioned from giving feedback to coaching, which is exactly as we would have wanted it to happen. She had the confidence to do it, too! She changed the way she thought about a feedback conversation – she had shifted her mindset.

A couple of weeks later, I heard from a senior vice president in the organization who knew I was coaching Natalie. She told me that people had seen a noticeable difference in Zach. It was like night and day; he was much more relaxed in meetings, was listening better, wasn't blurting out opinions, and was much more self-aware.

A manager's dread of giving feedback can derail the conversation before it even happens. Whenever you go into a situation in which you must deliver information that isn't positive, you need to take the time to get clear and establish a mindset for success. It's not just about facts. How you present the facts makes it possible for the recipient to be open to them, comprehend them, and, of course, take action. How you deliver the news and *how you prepare your mindset for the conversation* can have a tremendous impact on its outcome.

CHAPTER 7

SUMMARY

As we said at the beginning, to perform well or powerfully in the next level of your career, having professional and technical competence will not be enough. Combining these with your ability to examine, recognize, and shift your mindset (as needed) will be the key!

Our intention was to make a powerful case and to persuade you to examine how your mindset impacts your ability to be confident and grounded in high-stakes situations. There isn't a magic pill; only your fortitude and commitment to succeeding will make a difference. Keep trying different approaches. Start small and experiment when the stakes are low. Remember, it takes repetition and feedback to become unconsciously competent with these skills and techniques.

Even though we coach clients on how to shift their mindset, we are human too and often need to reflect and take our own coaching! On an almost daily basis, we find ourselves using these techniques, and every now and then, we will encourage each other to shift to a more positive and empowered mindset. In this book, we have mostly focused on building the muscle required to succeed in high-stakes business situations. We hope once you start shifting your mindset on a regular basis, you will feel the impact of it in ALL areas of your life, just as we have.

CHAPTER 8

AUTHORS' MINDSET MILESTONES

As we were writing this book, we often reflected on how we came to be so fascinated by the power of mindset. As we shared our personal stories, we realized that before we ever met, and certainly before we consciously thought about the concept of mindset, we were applying many of the concepts. We thought about our own high-stakes presentations, conversations, situations, and experiences and have decided to share them with you here.

Jeff Hornstein: How the Power of Mindset Revealed Itself

Milestone One

When I was coming up through the ranks in manufacturing, I don't think I ever heard the word *mindset*. I was a young engineer who had just become a training director, about one year into the role. I was good at my job and wanted to do what was best for the company and my peers.

Unfortunately, I found myself in a very unpleasant situation sitting in the plant manager's office while he berated me for nearly two, very intense hours. Had I not developed my ability to deliberately shift my mindset to an empowering place, I'm absolutely certain the outcome of that experience would have derailed my career. Here's what happened.

One day, I received a call from our division president who asked me to come to his office. He told me that he'd been hearing about quality problems within the tooling department.

He said to me, "I want you to go out there right away and teach these machinists how to drill a straight hole." I paused for a moment and thought to myself, *"Is he serious?"*

Then, I gathered my thoughts (and courage) and said, "Bob, with all due respect, I understand what you want me to do, but if I go out there and tell these guys how to drill a straight hole, they will likely feel insulted. It wouldn't surprise me if their response to me would be something like, 'What do you know about drilling or milling, you college punk? I've been a machinist for twenty years! I know what I'm doing; now waltz back up to your applications lab and leave us alone.'"

Then, I paused and waited for Bob to reply. He eventually asked me how I proposed to handle the issue. I told him I'd heard them complaining about equipment problems, outdated tooling, and that their boss always seemed to take forever to reply to their requests.

"It seems that what these people need is someone to ask them about their concerns, issues, and needs; listen to their requests; and then give them a timely response

— even if the response is a 'no.' Most importantly, we need to make sure they feel heard."

He reluctantly replied, "I don't think it will do any good but go ahead and get started."

So, I reached out to all the managers I needed to get permission from and began my task. Promising confidentiality, I reached out to each machinist, one at a time, and started to survey them. We met in the break room for coffee, and I asked questions about what they needed to improve quality.

The sessions were going well. As I got near the last one or two surveys, I received a call from someone whom I had completely forgotten to contact for permission: the plant manager. He asked me to come to his office right away!

My first thought was, "Holy moly, I can't believe I forgot to talk with him." After about thirty seconds, my next thoughts were about my commitment to confidentiality with the machinists and that their concerns would be heard. Following those thoughts, I thought about my responsibility to do what is best for the company and our customers. As a result, whatever the plant manager was going to say (or do) to me didn't really matter; I was confident I was doing the right thing.

As I sat down across from his desk, it took him no more than three seconds before he exploded. He blasted me, swearing and screaming that I had destroyed two years of intelligence work that his mole had been collecting. He went on and on for probably 40 minutes or so, before I could say anything. Finally, he stopped.

I apologized profusely and explained that I had gotten approval from everyone else and had assumed the machine shop manager had told him what we agreed to, but (obviously) that didn't happen, and I had made a terrible mistake in not seeking his permission.

After another 45 minutes or so of berating me, he finally stopped for a moment, and I jumped in and said, "You can keep yelling at me for as long as you want, but that is not going to solve our issue. I promised the machinists that management would reply to the surveys, and if that doesn't happen, things will only get worse."

He told me to get the heck out of his office and not to plan on going home for a while. As I walked back to my desk, I was thinking I was going to get fired. Preparing for that to happen, I wasn't surprised when I got a call from the head of HR asking me to come up to Mahogany Row (aka, the senior leadership team offices).

As I made my way up to the executive wing, I thought about the worst-case scenario. For the machinists, it would mean they would be even more distrustful of management. For me, it would mean looking for a new job.

Then, I thought about one possible saving grace. The vice president of manufacturing had agreed that once the surveying was complete, he would meet with the machinists and respond to their requests. If he'd keep his promise, it would at least give the machinists some hope that management actually did listen to them. Whether or not I'd still have a job was another matter.

As I walked into one of the plush, upscale offices, all six members of the senior leadership team (including the vice president of manufacturing) were standing and staring at me, as one of them asked me to take a seat. The questioning (that felt more like an interrogation) began with things like: What were you thinking? Who authorized this? How could you possibly…and so on.

I answered all the questions truthfully and figured the cards would fall however they were going to fall. Then, one of them asked about what I'd done with the information I had gathered. I told them I had it and had not shared it with anyone.

Another one of them asked me to send it to him. In that moment, I quickly reflected on the deliberate mindset I had created: Regardless of the consequences to me, I was going to do what I thought was right.

Realizing I was about to take a HUGE risk, I respectfully told them I had promised confidentiality to the machinists, and I would not break my agreement with them. Looking flabbergasted, they just stared at me in disbelief. I figured the ultimatum was next: "Hand over the file, or you're fired." Luckily, that didn't happen. Instead, they mumbled quietly to one another and finally told me to go back to my desk.

About two hours later, guess who called me? The vice president of manufacturing! We met for coffee the next morning and agreed he would, indeed, keep his commitment.

Flash forward about four weeks later, the vice president and I spent a lot of time planning the meeting with the machinists. In the end, those meetings went better than expected. The team of machinists got to spend three hours talking with the vice president about what was on their wish list. While not all the items were purchased, enough were. As a result, the machinists felt as if they had finally been heard, and morale and quality improved.

This could have gone in a completely different direction had the vice president not stepped up, taken a risk to stick his neck out, and agreed to hold that meeting with the machinists.

Without the ability to create the deliberate mindset I felt was needed for that situation, I cannot possibly fathom how I would have dealt with the fear and concern that could have prevented me from keeping my commitments. This is when I began to identify the idea of and power in creating a deliberate mindset. As I began to use this new tool, my life began to change in such a positive way...it was mind-blowing!

Milestone Two

After delivering day one of a two-day intensive workshop to a group of driven sales professionals, my colleague and I decided to enjoy a nice dinner and stroll around the streets of Georgetown. We spent about an hour talking about changes we wanted to make for the second day. As we were wrapping up and heading toward our respective hotel rooms, I said to my colleague, "I'm going to spend time tonight meditating and creating a mindset of gratitude and prosperity which, by the way, will lead to me meeting someone in the health club tomorrow morning who we will end up doing business with."

She looked at me and said, "Huh? Good luck with that." Her tone and facial expression clearly indicated she thought I had consumed too much wine during dinner! We said goodnight and agreed to meet for breakfast.

How was I able to make such a bold statement, let alone have the confidence that it would happen? The answer is actually simple: I made the shift from a default to a deliberate mindset.

For a long time without realizing it, I had been living with a strong default mindset of scarcity. From fifth grade through somewhere in my late twenties, I often felt constrained and thought very little about what could be possible. Living with that mindset in place, my life was going to be pretty predictable.

That began to change after I met a man named Doug Robertson. We had known one another for a few years but were only acquaintances. At some point, we started having more meaningful conversations, and he became a great friend and mentor. Doug suggested I consider this: Much more was possible for me than I could even imagine.

As our friendship deepened, Doug continued to ask me more about my thoughts that originated from a place of scarcity. As a result of our conversations I really started to question those thoughts. That inquiry and my trust in

Doug led me to explore and to want to dig deeper. My quest to see if and how I could shift away from the scarcity mindset to one of gratitude and prosperity was put into motion.

From that inquiry, my life started to change, and I found myself in places I hadn't been before. I began desiring and having more meaningful conversations with people. I started reading books on personal growth, participating in workshops, and meditating – trying to absorb all that I could, as long as it revolved around shifting my mindset to a powerful and positive place. These days, I've added listening to podcasts and watching YouTube videos to that list!

The next morning at 6:00 a.m., my alarm went off. As I was getting ready to head to the health club, I noticed my thoughts were about riding on the recumbent bike, not on the deliberate mindset I created the night before, which shows how hard it is to sustain! As I walked in, I saw only one recumbent bike in the club, and it was being used by another gentleman. While he was pedaling, I noticed he was reading *USA Today.*

I decided to strike up a conversation, so I asked if he was there for business or pleasure.

He said, "Just working out before I get to the office."

He asked the same question of me, and I replied that I was on business getting ready for the second day of a program I was delivering. He asked what type of program it was, and I replied that it was a presentation skills type of class (which is now known as *Communicating Credibility*).

He then paused and said, "Hmm, tell me more about this class of yours."

I described it at a high level and summed it up by saying, "We essentially teach people how to stand up straight, look people in the eye, and not to say *um*!"

This seemed to pique his interest. He asked more questions:

"What would you do if you had smart people on your team pitching to your prospective clients, but they won't stop talking?"

"Some of our people take what seems like thirty minutes to get to the point. Do you have techniques to help them?"

"We've got people on our team who are passionate, but it isn't always obvious to clients. Can you help with that issue?"

After about ten minutes or so, he said, "Nice talking with you; good luck with your session today."

With a deliberate mindset of gratitude and prosperity in my mind, I remembered telling myself: "The time is now to GO FOR IT." So, I said, "It seemed like you were interested in what we do – I'd love to follow up with you. I can run back to my room and grab a business card."

He responded, "No, I need to get showered but look me up on our website and send me an e-mail; my name is Jim Clifton."

I asked what company he worked for, and he told me: Gallup. Then I asked what his role was.

He said, "I'm the chairman and CEO." Wow, talk about the power of my intention!

We shook hands, wished one another a good day, and I told him I'd reach out to him later that morning and send him an e-mail. After finishing my workout, I met my colleague for breakfast and told her about the conversation that had taken place at the hotel gym.

She said, "You were lucky to be in the right place at the right time." What my coworker had called *luck*, I would call *an opportunity manifested through deliberate mindset.*

Flashing forward, after exchanging a series of emails with Mr. Clifton and some of the managing directors, our company was later given the chance to work with some of their folks. We were very excited for the opportunity! That initial workshop went very well and has led to a long relationship and many prosperous engagements.

If this is what happened to me, what could be possible for you?

Sue Reynolds-Frost: Determination and Growth Fueled by Mindset

Milestone One

Like Jeff, I was creating deliberate mindsets before I knew the term *mindset*. When I think about how I grew into my career as a coach and leadership development professional, I can confidently say that much of my determination and growth was fueled by the power of what I now know to be *mindset*.

My story is not necessarily unique in terms of standard career growth. What I hope to convey is the power you can have by creating deliberate mindsets at pivotal moments. The choices I made and the opportunities I seized were directly correlated to my ability to sustain the practice of consciously choosing my attitude and mindset.

When I was twenty-six years old, I was determined to change my career path from marketing to training. I was working as a marketing assistant for a not-for-profit organization. It was the second job I had of this nature, and (like in my previous job) after about a year, I found myself restless. I was eager and wanted more responsibility. I asked my boss if I could attend a training class to learn more about designing marketing materials. He agreed, and a week later I was sitting in a three-day desktop publishing class. Little did I know that this class would change the course of my career.

After the first thirty minutes of the class, I found myself mesmerized…not by the content but by Patricia, our instructor. I loved how she commanded control in front of the room, how she engaged with all of us, how she infused humor, and how masterful she was at teaching us how to use the software application. I could see myself doing what she did!

I was a quick study with software, and I enjoyed speaking in front of people. Even though I didn't have any experience, I knew I could do it, and that deliberate mindset gave me the confidence to approach Patricia at the end of our last day. I asked her, "How did you become a trainer?" She told me about her technical background and experience as a teacher earlier in her career.

I said, "I'd like to do what you do. Is your company hiring?" She replied, "We're always looking for good trainers. What experience do you have?"

I remember in that moment thinking to myself: I'm going to go for it, so I said, "Even though I don't have any technical training experience, I know I can do this."

She just looked at me kindly and said, "Well, dear, I'm sure over time you probably could become a trainer. I recommend that you get certified in some of the software applications we teach, and then, perhaps, I could introduce you to our hiring manager." She then gave me her business card and told me to keep in touch.

As I rode the train home that evening, I kept thinking that all I had to do was get some time in front of her to show her: I was a quick study, and I could do this job. I called her not once, but five times over the course of the next three weeks. (Note – this is pre-email days, folks!)

Finally, she returned my call and said, "Well, you certainly are persistent. I can't introduce you to my hiring manager until I have a sense of your skills."

I said, "I understand completely. I'd like to present a training module to you – fifteen minutes is all I need."

She invited me to visit her in her classroom after her next workshop. I had the distinct feeling she was doing this merely to get me to stop bothering her. Nevertheless, I felt confident.

I was hired as a trainer a few weeks later, then was subsequently promoted to senior trainer and office manager for one of their satellite offices, and was extremely fulfilled during the three years I worked there. When I look back, my ability to create a deliberate mindset of "I can do this!" gave me the confidence to pursue and secure a job for which I had absolutely no prior experience. It also propelled me through the rigor of learning more than fifty software applications and being able to stand in front of groups as a subject matter expert.

It doesn't mean that I never had doubts or that I wasn't nervous about standing in front of people. Whenever I experienced those feelings of uncertainty, I would call on my mantra, "I can do it!" and would repeat it in my mind to drown out the negative noise that was self-limiting. It worked and continues to work for me to this day.

Milestone Two

About three years into my role as a software trainer, I was recruited into Spencer Stuart, one of the world's top executive search firms. I was hired to help roll out the firm's proprietary database, a new challenge and one that took me around the world. These were some of the best times of my life – in fact, I met my husband, Angus, while working there. I literally have Spencer Stuart to thank for my amazing family!

About eighteen months into the job, I had that familiar, restless feeling again. At that point in my life, I was reading about self-awareness and emotional intelligence and attending a variety of professional development workshops. I knew I wasn't going to be satisfied focusing on technology training forever but also knew our firm did not have many opportunities for me beyond that role. I was feeling discouraged and didn't know what my options were; I just knew my passions resided outside of the realm of technology.

I had just attended a workshop that focused on creating possibilities for my life, and I walked away with a new set of ideas and tools to help me generate a positive mindset for the task ahead: to reinvent my role within the training team. I had a sense of calm resolve, an inner-knowledge that I could (and would) do this! That mindset gave me the confidence to set the wheels in motion, and it started with asking my boss, Mary Kay, if I could get certified in the Myers-Briggs Type Indicator (MBTI). I am eternally grateful that Mary Kay was so supportive of my career development and equally motivated to expand our team's impact on the firm. She was a true mentor in every sense of the word.

This certification paved the way for us to start offering a few interpersonal effectiveness programs. Like Jeff, the body of literature and personal growth programs I was immersed in during this time introduced me more formally to the power of mindset. I knew the firm needed this type of content, and I was convinced our team could make an impact. My mindset was set: We could do this – no matter how long it took!

After several attempts (some of which failed), we started running some of the firm's functional, new hire programs – a BIG win for our group. As with many internal training functions, proving relevance and credibility to our various audiences was challenging; we knew we needed an advocate and champion for our efforts. Fortunately, one of our adjunct faculty members and partners in the firm, Liane, threw her hat in the ring to become the head of professional development for the firm. She got the job, and the firm's first-ever professional development function was born.

Liane taught me so much about persistence, agility, and having high standards – no matter what the cost. During that period, we had to persuade, convince, cajole, and gain buy-in from numerous partners. With every meeting, proposal, and effort, I had to keep checking my mindset – moving away from discouragement and impatience toward empowerment and confidence.

Milestone Three

About ten years into my role at Spencer Stuart, I was at a different crossroads. My first daughter, Meredith, was two years old, and I found myself pregnant with twins! Throughout the course of my pregnancy, I was focused on one thing and one thing only: bringing those babies safely into the world. I also started thinking about what it would be like to juggle work and three kids under the age of three. Knowing I needed to figure out how to handle three kids in diapers, I took about a year off to focus on my young family.

When I started getting the itch to go back to work, I wanted a new challenge. I wanted to be client-facing rather than internally focused. This was around 2008, and we all remember what a great year that was for business...especially for people in coaching/training/professional development. Companies were cutting back drastically on training, and trying to start a new practice seemed impossible.

Like many others in my field, I started networking and meeting other sole practitioners in the training and development world. I managed to develop a couple of great client relationships and recognized quickly that I would prefer to team up with a colleague rather than go it alone. While I had no idea how I would find this collaboration partner, I knew that I would.

I started imagining what type of person I wanted to work with. This person would have to share the same values that I had, have a similar approach to coaching and helping people grow in their careers, and have an authentic/genuine character. Little did I know that I was practicing one of the techniques we talk about in the book – *Envision a Future State*! It was then that I was introduced to Jeff Hornstein.

I quickly learned that Jeff embodied the characteristics I imagined. I started collaboratiing with him about six months later, and this journey began. Not only do we have complementary styles, but we are both committed to helping our clients become the best versions of themselves, in any way we can. We support and help one another shift our own mindsets (when needed) and have also become great friends.

When he asked me to partner with him on writing this book on mindset, I was all in. In every workshop we deliver and every coaching engagement we participate in, we integrate the power of mindset. It made perfect sense that we then would collaborate to write a book sharing our passion for this work, combined practical experiences, and recommendations for how to take control of mindset to make it in high-stakes situations.

As I reflect on the arduous process of writing this book, I am reminded of the many times both Jeff and I had to shift our mindsets: from overwhelmed to engaged, discouraged to encouraged, or simply from tired to energized! Time and again, we leveraged the exact tools we espouse in these chapters, because they work! It's not always easy to be willing to shift out of a disempowering mindset; the momentum associated with negative thoughts can feel as strong as a heavy current in a raging river. Your willingness to stop and examine your thoughts is the first and often most powerful step. We hope that you are willing to take that step!

SUGGESTED AUTHORS AND THOUGHT LEADERS

Below is a short list of some of our favorite thought leaders, teachers, and gurus on all subjects related to emotional intelligence and personal empowerment. We have learned so much from reading their works, listening to them, and (in some cases) participating in their programs. Many of their beliefs and teachings are integrated into the heart of the work we do every day.

- Brene Brown, Ph.D.
- Deepak Chopra, M.D.
- Amy Cuddy, Ph.D.
- Dr. Wayne Dyer
- Marshall Goldsmith, Ph.D.
- Daniel Goleman, Ph.D.
- Judith E. Glaser
- Esther Hicks and Jerry Hicks
- Napoleon Hill
- Dr. Carl Jung
- Landmark Education
- Daniel J. Levitan, Ph.D.
- Pathways to Successful Living Seminars
- Bob Proctor

- Mel Robbins
- Tony Robbins
- Karlin Sloan
- Andrew Sobel
- Douglas Stone
- Eckhart Tolle
- Larry Wilson
- Jon Kabat Zin, Ph.D.

APPENDIX

Here's a one-stop shop for all the techniques and models we described in the book for a quick reference guide.

3-Step Process
(Page 17)

1. **Discover your default mindset** – What is holding you back?

2. **Decide to shift your mindset** – Choose to move toward something positive.

3. **Create a deliberate mindset** – Choose the best technique to help you shift.

Step 1: Tools to Uncover Default Mindsets That Are Holding You Back
(Pages 21-26)

The first step is uncovering possible default mindsets that might be influencing you.

1. **Examine your complaints** – Find default mindsets based on the things you complain about the most.

2.   **Listen to feedback** – Find a board of directors, people you can trust to give you reliable feedback. Listen to the feedback they give and respond accordingly.

3.   **Reflect** – See things from another perspective. Put yourself in someone else's shoes. Think about your actions from another point of view.

4.   **Identify grudges** – Built up over time, grudges are often the source of negative, default mindsets.

Step 2: Decide to Shift Your Mindset
(Pages 28-32)

Once you've become conscious of a default mindset, you need to make a choice to do something about it.

1.   **Find an accountability partner** – To help ensure success, find an outside influence to nudge or push you the extra mile.

2.   **Envision a future state** – Create a mental image of what the future state looks and feels like.

3.   **Write it down** – People support what they create. Track your progress and solidify your goals.

Step 3: Create a Deliberate Mindset
(Pages 35-70)

Now it's time for action. Determine the approaches and techniques that will help you create a deliberate and more powerful mindset.

The key to mastering new skills and behaviors is practice. The four levels of competence model provides a way to understand this process.

1. **Acknowledge your emotions** – Take a serious look at your emotions and how they might link to a default mindset that isn't serving you.

2. **Stop-Challenge-Choose** – Prevent your emotions/
    feelings from driving your reactions when faced with
    high-stakes presentations and conversations.

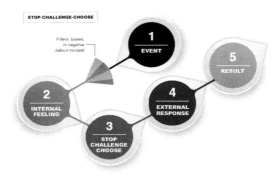

3. **Pause and Breathe**

> Breathe in for four counts, hold your breath in
> for four counts, breathe out for four counts, and
> then hold for four counts. Repeat several times.
> IMPACT: Focuses your attention away from
> nerves AND has the calming effect of lowering
> cortisol and decreasing the heart rate.

4. **24-Hour Rule** – If it is a high-stakes situation, and
    you have the opportunity to buy yourself time
    before engaging or making a decision, we suggest
    waiting 24 hours before you do anything.

5. **Find Another Way to Say It** – Whether you
    relieve stress by venting to co-workers, or you just
    have a nasty internal dialogue about something,
    our strong suggestion would be to find another
    way to say it.

6. **Pick a Mantra** – Think of a quick phrase or saying that can get you unhooked quickly if you feel yourself drifting into a negative spiral before a high-stakes situation.

7. **Laugh** – Laughter is not only good for shifting your mindset in the moment, but it helps you remember not to take life or yourself too seriously.

8. **Meditate** – The benefits of this technique are cumulative. Pick a technique that helps you to quiet your mind.

9. **Point of View Model** – Your truth is not the only truth. Are you willing to consider other viewpoints?

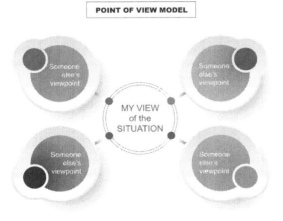

POINT OF VIEW MODEL

Someone else's viewpoint

Someone else's viewpoint

MY VIEW of the SITUATION

Someone else's viewpoint

Someone else's viewpoint

10. **Create a Game** – Create a game to shift your mindset away from diminishing, negative thoughts.

If you want more information on The Speaker's Choice Communicating Credibility™ programs, go to **TheSpeakersChoice.com** or contact Jeff at Jeff@thespeakerschoice.com.

If you want learn more about Sue's executive coaching services, workshops or leadership development consulting, go to **reynfro.com** or contact her at Sreynoldsfrost@reynfro.com.

51824527R00085

Made in the USA
Columbia, SC
22 February 2019